How to Start and Produce
a Magazine or Newsletter

First published 1986 by Cromarty Press, Sydney, as How to Start and Produce a Magazine — a comprehensive guide. ISBN 0 949675 16 4
Second edition, substantially revised, by The Worsley Press, initially of Wangaratta, in 1991, then Rutherglen, as How to Start and Produce a Magazine (or Newspaper). ISBN 0 646 05684 0. Reprinted with minor revisions 1995.
Third edition (fully revised and updated): as How to Start and Produce a Magazine or Newsletter ISBN 1 875750 15 0 published June 2000 reprinted 2002

This fourth edition revised and updated ISBN 1 875750 21 5 published 2004

The Worsley Press
11 Lintel Court
Hastings
Victoria 3915
Australia
info@worsleypress.com
ABN 90 642 570 141

Distributed in the USA by:
FAP Books Inc.
PO Box 540
Gainesville FL 32602

Distributed in the UK by:
Eyelevel Books
2 Crutch Farm Bungalow,
Elmbridge, Droitwich,
WR9 0BG, England

© Gordon Woolf, 1986, 1991, 2000, 2004

Other books by Gordon Woolf:
    Success in Store (with Geoffrey Heard)
    Publication Production using PageMaker
    Publish Your Book
    How to Produce a Newspaper using PageMaker 4 (under Windows 3.0)
    PC-Style: a stylebook that you can personalise (revised as Stylebook)
    How to Buy, Run and Sell a Milk Bar
    The Manager's Guide to DOS
    Newspaper Production using PageMaker 5
    Newspaper Production using PageMaker 6.5

The National Library of Australia Cataloguing-in-Publication entry:
Woolf, Gordon. 1941-
    How to start and produce a magazine or newsletter
    4th ed.
    Includes index.
    ISBN 1 875750 21 5
    1. Newsletters - Publishing. 2. Periodicals. Publishing.
    I. Woolf, Gordon, 1941- How to start and produce a magazine
    (or newspaper). II. Title.
    070.572

BISAC: Publishing LAN027000; Small Business BUS060000; Desktop Publishing COM022000

This book is copyright. Apart from any fair dealing for the purpose of private study, research, criticism or review as permitted under the Copyright Act, no part may be reproduced, stored in a retrieval system, or transmitted in any form or by any means without prior written permission from the publisher at the address above, phone (03) 5979 1112 or email info@worsleypress.com. Copying for educational purposes is permitted to the extent allowed under the Copyright Act 1968 provided that that educational institution or the body that administers it has given a remuneration notice to Copyright Agency Limited (CAL) under this Act (For details contact CAL by phone (02) 9394 7600 or email info@copyright.com.au)

Set by The Worsley Press in Garamond Pro using Adobe InDesign. Printed in Australia by Ligare Pty Ltd, Riverwood

HOW TO START AND PRODUCE A MAGAZINE OR NEWSLETTER

Fourth Edition

by
Gordon Woolf

The Worsley Press

More information

On our web site you will find contacts for more information on publishing in general and on the publishing of formatted publications such as newsletters, magazines and newspapers.

You will also find any corrections and updates to this book and you can subscribe to our *Format* newsletter which is distributed about once a month.

We also invite e-mail comments and will try to answer any further questions you may have.

Your private website for this book is at:

http://www.worsleypress.com/magbook-private

which requires the following to enter:

username: magbook4

password: mb2004

Our general publication production website is at:

http://www.worsleypress.com/pubprod/

and you will find much general information freely available there.

About the Author

Gordon Woolf is the author of a wide range of books on publishing, editing, desktop publishing and small business. He is the principal of The Worsley Press, through which he publishes his own books and a selected range of other titles. Gordon is a consultant to small newspapers and magazines world-wide. He became editor of his first magazine as a teenager and over four decades has published magazines in the fields of music, farm machinery, unions, photography and entertainment as well as working for some of the smallest and largest publishers in England and Australia. Gordon has also been involved in the retail trade and gained an insight into the practical side of magazine sales through a bookshop and convenience store.

Contents

Introduction

A lot more than laying out pages

This book will be invaluable to the hands-on magazine or newsletter publisher — the person starting or running a magazine or newsletter who will take on a major active role in all aspects of management and production. The person in a management role in a larger publishing organization will also find it useful in assisting them to understand the processes and what other people are doing.

There is a lot more to producing a magazine or newsletter than knowing how to lay out pages on a computer, so this is not a computer book. It certainly includes a goodly number of hints on how to use your computer to produce a magazine or newsletter. But it is not intended to take the place of whatever manuals came with your desktop publishing program.

It *is* intended to help with all the problems computer manuals do not cover … everything you need to know to plan and produce your own publication.

As you will see, there is much more to producing a publication than just the physical task of arranging words and pictures on paper. That is why, although this book was first published before desktop publishing became the norm, there is much that remains virtually unchanged.

However, for this fourth edition, substantial parts of the chapters on the physical side of production have been rewritten despite being previously completely rewritten for the third edition — and the book has again grown in length.

Changed roles of printer and publisher

Power to do the job badly

Much that used to be a printer's job is now in the hands of the publication staff — be it fully-paid professional staff or the lone amateur editor. Desktop publishing — the ability to have the basic equipment for producing a publication within a package costing just a few thousand dollars — has meant that there are many more publications around.

It has also meant that there are many bad publications around. We now have even greater power to do the job badly!

But why a publication at all?

Everyone wants to know what is going on in any field that concerns them, whether it is the world at large or the local football club.

The committee of every club will, at some stage, consider producing some form of magazine or newsletter to keep the members informed

— often to correct the misinformation produced by the notoriously unreliable word-of-mouth system.

Similarly, every company employing more than a handful of staff, or with more than a few dozen customers may consider how it will keep in touch with those customers, and a newsletter or house magazine is one of the more cost effective solutions.

Chore or an exciting job?

To someone will fall the task of producing the newsletter. If that someone is you, will it become a chore or can it be an exciting job? For me, publications have always represented excitement. At school, it was a wall-newspaper, with each column typed individually on an ancient upright Imperial which had a letter 't' that had dropped and looked like a '+' sign.

When I started work, my hobby, as a not-very-good jazz musician, took on a new importance when I became the teenage editor of a duplicated magazine for local musicians.

Editorial duties extended to turning the handle on the well-worn manual Gestetner duplicator to produce the few hundred copies. Then, at work, I added to my stores clerk job the duties of editor of the properly printed staff association magazine.

Magazines and zines

Amateur enthusiasm and lateness

That initial music magazine was little different to the many "zines" which grew out of the fan magazines of that era. "Zine" is sometimes described as an abbreviation of "magazine" but it is more often described as coming from "fanzine" which was itself a merging of the words "fan magazine" typified by the many magazines put out by official and unofficial fan clubs of musicians, groups, singers, etc. in the 1960s to 1980s. What they had in common was an amateur enthusiasm and a tendency for that to result in each issue being later than the previous one. Photocopying led to a boom in such magazines: photocopy the A4 or Letter size sheets, fold them, staple them, and there was a "real" magazine.

In my own progress, we found a printer for our home-produced magazine, and by a process more like Topsy than a business plan, the hobby publication changed shape, title and readership to become a demanding small-circulation trade journal that was read throughout the world, and took me overseas frequently. It even had sections in German and Italian, languages I do not pretend to understand. To keep up I had to leave my "day job" (I had by then moved on to a farming magazine).

Since that time I have published and/or edited magazines about music and photography, and one that listed 'What's On' details for Sydney. I have edited a country town newspaper and a group of regional newspapers bringing out a paper every day, and have run a small-offset printing plant. I have been chief sub-editor for a group of suburban newspapers and a sub-editor on two of Australia's largest-circulation magazines. I have trained the staff of several provincial newspapers in production using desktop publishing methods and, more recently, bought, run and sold, a small-town newspaper. I have also handled the layout and production of a wide range of small, and not-so-small, publications. In combination with that I ran a business training in publication production and looking at means of improving publication methods.

In those several decades of publishing, the methods of production have ranged from typing stencils to handling page make-up on a computer. I have turned the handle on a duplicator and operated a printing press, set type by hand, Linotype, IBM Composer and by mainframe and desktop computer, as well as pasting-up page layouts, both physically and on screen, and making plates.

Excitement of a new edition

They are never perfect

Still there is an excitement with every new edition. They are never perfect, but each improves the next. As a journalist, I enjoy writing, but I enjoy the production of a publication more. I also realized in the early stages of my writing career that it mattered little how good the words are if the publication does not get printed and distributed in time to reach the readers for whom it is intended. Their reaction is what really matters and which provides the satisfaction, enjoyment and justification for what is printed. I hope in this book to pass on some of that enjoyment and to explain some of the short cuts I have found along the way.

To provide some sequence to the book, we will look at what may be a small social club newsletter and follow its growth through systems suited to progressively larger circulations. We will consider how a first issue of a new publication for a small group of specialists might be planned. Then we will deal with the problems of economics and distribution, whether by subscription or through newsstands and other retail outlets on a national or even international basis. We will also look at the most recent of magazine productions, the "e-zine" distributed via the Internet, at its simpler cousin, the e-mail newsletter, and at ways of creating a "web presence" for a print publication.

May I also suggest that this is the kind of book which you may need to scan through on many occasions after reading it a first time. There is likely to be information which will not be of interest at first, but which will become very important as you enter other stages of publication production.

Since magazine production is a highly interactive affair, it is also likely there will be valuable information about topics in sections other than those which deal principally with those topics. In many cases these are cross referenced by margin notes. The production of magazines or newsletters consists of many interrelated tasks and small actions in one area may have a major effect on other aspects of the production.

Watch and learn

Even though you may be concerned with only one part of the production, it helps greatly to know what happens to your work in other parts of the process. Therefore take every opportunity to visit service bureaus, printing plants, and the offices and production areas of other publications. Everything you see will help you understand the total process and how the stages meld together for smooth production. You may also see how you could take shortcuts which may make the work easier.

The thought of growing your own publication from a photocopied news-sheet to a nationally or internationally circulating magazine is not so far fetched as you might think. It is the way my first magazine grew and it is how others are growing magazines today.

Chapter 1

The first steps

Correcting rumors

Almost every organization of any size either has a magazine or would like to have one. It can help keep an organization together — keeping members who cannot attend every meeting in touch with what is going on and introducing personalities to new members so that they feel more at home. It can remind those present at meetings of what was agreed and can encourage participation by detailing more about plans than can be given while maintaining a high level of attention.

Even in a business where everyone is in contact every day, a newsletter can be valuable. It can help explain company decisions in simple terms, maintaining goodwill and enthusiasm. It can also be used to correct rumors before they reach damaging proportions. In a similar way, such a journal can maintain contact between a business and its customers.

Need not be expensive

A newsletter or magazine need not be expensive to produce, although the importance of such publications is indicated by the high level of spending on internal house journals (to employees) and external ones (to customers) by many major companies. They maintain them even, perhaps especially, during periods when other departments are faced with major economies. Such points indicate the importance of a magazine or newsletter, but how do you set about starting one?

The first trade magazine

Let us say the social club meets every month. It is likely that many members would forget just when unless they receive a reminder a few days before. While you are sending out a notice, you may like to add a few notes about what is going to happen and reports on what has happened. It could be just a photocopied sheet, but if you give it a title, you have the beginnings of a publication. In fact the very first trade magazines were catalogues published by a London chemist who added articles to ensure they were read.

Registration seldom needed

I am often asked whether a magazine has to be registered in some way. The simple answer for most countries is no — that is one of the cornerstones of free expression. If you wish you may register the title with the post office, and possibly benefit from reduced postage rates — and postage is one of the major costs facing any organization.

You may also like to register the title as a business name, which, while it does not actually protect your title it may be enough of a disincentive and will stop others from trading under that name at least in your state.

More on legal aspects — page 179

You may also be required by law to send a copy of each issue to a State or National library.

Covering costs with advertisements

Genuine or a tax deduction

Once you have a publication you also open up the prospect of covering some of the costs with advertisements. Some advertisements may be genuine — the members probably spend money on their activity and the businesses that cover that activity know that they will gain goodwill and sales by showing that they support the club. Other advertisements may just be members willing to put money into the club in a way that they can show as a tax deduction.

We will look at ways of getting advertisements into a small publication in the chapters that cover methods of production, from photocopying to the many forms of printing. Also we will look at the general field of advertisements and give guidelines on working out an economic rate — a problem that can tax the brain of even the best cost accountant.

More on adverts — page 39

If you are producing a magazine which is to stand on its own feet financially, either as a business enterprise, or as a self-financing adjunct to a club, you do have to consider whether there is enough potential advertisement revenue in that field. For example, while there is plenty of advertising revenue in individual sports activities, most general sports magazines worldwide have failed to find sufficient advertisers interested in reaching those generally interested in sports.

Making decisions: committee or editor

Is it a camel?

You have almost certainly been told that a camel is a horse designed by a committee, and few good magazines have come from a committee system. Therefore, while your committee or board should set down general guidelines for the publication (when it should appear, general content, the budget, and so on), the responsibility should go to one person to ensure it comes out.

Even the smallest publication requires a lot of decisions to be taken instantly, so there is good reason for the general system of the editor having full responsibility for content. If decisions have to be referred to other people you will soon find that the April issue comes out in May.

What is required in an editor? More than anything else he or she needs to be a well-balanced individual, who may well get enthused by a project but who will also be able to look at it with a certain detachment and to listen to the views of others.

In some publications such as club and house journals and company newsletters, there is often a need to set out clearly just how much "editing" the editor can do on submissions. Do you have the right to change items submitted by the CEO or chairman? Are you required to submit edited articles to their authors? Most major magazines will only do this under pressure and only for correction of factual errors. Whatever the policy for your publication, make sure that it is clearly set out in advance.

An editor needs to be a good organiser, knowing that many of those items promised so enthusiastically are not likely to appear on time, if at all. He or she will have other items in hand to take their place, so that deadlines can be met without panic. He or she does not have to be a great writer although a reasonable command of basic English is essential.

You may never have heard of logistics, but since I met a logistics expert, I've found it is what publishers and editors have to do all the time — making sure that dozens, sometimes hundreds, of items from widely disparate sources arrive at the place they are needed just as they are needed.

More on the job of an editor — page 21

Legally, what is needed is a large degree of common sense: though our laws of defamation and libel are confusing and can apply to the smallest publication as easily as the largest, problems will be avoided if common sense principles of not saying things which will offend are applied. If you really want to make a point that is critical of a person then firstly get legal advice, though my chapter on the legal side, with its mention of libel, does give some general guidelines.

The first step

An idea is not enough

Firstly, let us clarify one common misconception about magazine publishing. It is seldom possible to come up with an idea for a publication and sell that idea to a publisher. It just does not happen that way.

Even if you are an acknowledged expert in a field without a magazine, and you approach a publisher to start something for that readership, do not expect to have much say other than as a "consulting editor", a nominal role.

In fact, the larger existing publishers do not have a very good track record at starting magazines. They tend to buy publications which have been started by individuals and become successful. There are exceptions, but the life cycle of a magazine tends to be that it is started on a shoestring by an enthusiast, grows beyond their capability to cope with the increasing need for capital, despite generating a healthy profit, and so is taken over by a publishing company, under which it may exist healthily for years before its gradual decline.

More on the need for capital — page 163

It is also true that magazines and newsletters can be started on very little capital, since, in their simplest form they need just sufficient to pay for printing and distribution until the advertisement and sales revenue comes in. Equipment can be little more than a computer and telephone plus the furniture to put them on. Even so many people underestimate even the small capital needed, and it is almost impossible to persuade any normal financial institution to put up money for a magazine. There are just no assets sufficient to protect their investment. Therefore, if the magazine you are starting isn't being financed by an existing organization or business as it is for an in-house publication, then it is either your house on the line or you are dependent on family and friends.

Getting started

Collect examples

So, you have decided or have been asked to start a newsletter or magazine. How do you go about it?

It is not a bad idea to collect examples of publications from other organizations. It does not matter what the subject is, you just want examples to show around and to help decide the style which most suits your purpose.

Then you need to decide how much of the work you will do yourself, how much will be done by people in your immediate control (which can include employing specialists or finding the expertise within your organization) and how much will be contracted out.

For example, to create a newsletter in an existing business, you may decide to do all the planning and organization yourself, and to seek someone with existing word processing and computer skills to run the material you collect into a template file. It may be printed on the inhouse photocopier or taken to a quick-print centre and everyone pitches in to get them enveloped or labelled and ready to post.

More on using service bureaus etc — page 75

On the other hand it may require seeking out the services of a service bureau or graphic designer. Look at the colophon (the box where details of staff, printer and other vital information are located) in other publications: they often list the person or business which does the page layout.

While all graphic design firms can do magazine layout, the ones which specialize in that field will have workflow systems in place which considerably reduce costs. Specialist magazine printers may also know of design and layout businesses through their contacts with them. It is not

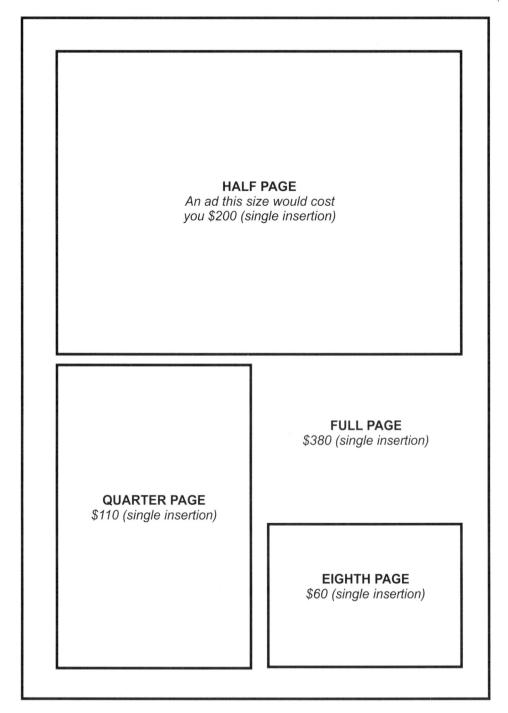

Fig.1-1: An idea for an advertisement leaflet which shows sizes and prices of ads visually. Watch as would-be advertisers start to sketch in what they want — and you will know you've made a sale!

unknown for a publication to handle page layouts in house but to contract out advertisement typesetting and special design work. In this way you can make use of trade expertise and still plan to gradually move towards doing all the page layout yourself or to having it done by people you employ.

Pre-publication issue

Dummy or pilot issue

Large-scale publishers often produce a dummy issue — a complete magazine with full editorial content. The publishers will also pick specimen advertisements from the clients they expect to get as advertisers and put those in at no charge. It is an expensive operation — after all the main cost (typesetting, artwork, printing plates) of a publication is to produce the first copy, so the cost of producing a few hundred will be very close to the cost of printing many thousands — and there is no revenue on a dummy.

A more recent approach has been to produce a pre-publication or pilot issue, with almost everything that will appear in a normal issue, but maybe a little thinner, and with some paid-for advertisements. This would go on sale for a couple of months before the real first issue and would be sent to all prospective advertisers. Such an issue could also be included free of charge with another publication in a related field, or perhaps with the newsletters of clubs and associations which cater for people with the magazine's interests.

On a smaller scale, I have found it very effective to produce a dummy cover with just the two inside cover pages carrying articles, in the editorial style that will be used, telling about the content and aims of the publication. The back cover could show the advertisement rates.

Talking to printers

Small changes can save dollars

The specimen copies of other magazines also enable you to talk to printers to see what formats suit their equipment. Often a change of a few millimetres in size can produce dramatic reductions in cost. But more of that later. Suffice to say now that it does not pay to have too firm a view of what you want before you start talking to printers.

It also pays to have a general understanding of how the printing system works. There are many books which explain this and I have seen some of the best non-technical explanations in books intended for children.

Almost all the printing you encounter will be based on offset-lithography. This printing system works in both small offset and in large newspaper and magazine presses, on the well known principle that oil and water do not mix. The image is greasy so when a damp roller passes over the plate, the non-image area is left damp, but the water is repelled by the image. Then when the ink roller passes over the plate, the greasy ink is repelled by the damp non-image area but sticks to the image.

The image from the plate, which is positive, then rolls on to a roller, usually covered with a rubber-like material which is known as a blanket, and from this (which is a reversed image) it rolls on to the paper to become a positive image again. Because it is not printed directly but is "offset" via the blanket, the whole process is known as offset, short for offset-lithography.

The lithographic process of printing is not only the most modern, it is also the oldest. High quality lithographs are still produced by a development of the stone-age principle of drawing with greasy materials on a stone, wetting the surface, rolling with ink and then rolling paper across.

Some presses will print from a web (the roll of paper) and will collate and fold automatically in the one process so that what comes out at the end of the press is a complete newspaper. A magazine then requires only stapling, called stitching in the trade, and a final trim.

More about talking to printers in Chapter 7 — page 63

With other presses, the paper will be in sheets, and the process is known as sheet-fed. The printed sheets have to go to separate machines for folding and collating, before being stitched and trimmed.

Surveys

Asking for opinions

"Let's put a reader survey in the next issue, to find out what the readers want!" To my mind this is like governments forming a committee: it gives the appearance of doing something without actually having to take any possibly unpopular decisions. Surveys have to be exceptionally well designed to get useful answers and can be designed to produce mostly the answers those setting the questions want to get.

Asking for opinions is unlikely to produce useful results, but if you want to get some factual answers then multiple choice questions and those which produce yes/no answers could work, particularly if asked by independent questioners.

I recall one such survey included with a magazine I subscribed to in the publishing field. In a question on what other publications I read, it listed a number of publications, one of which I had not come across. I found out more about that one, got a copy, decided I liked it better, and did not renew the one asking the questions. I'm sure that wasn't what they hoped to achieve! I wondered also if it was that new magazine which had the older one worried, and whether the survey had been their response.

Talk to people

In another of my books I quote successful and wealthy businessman Dick Smith who, after major success in retail, started the magazine *Australian*

Geographic which was forecast by many to fail but which was a dramatic success. His comment: "Talking to your staff and customers will soon tell you what your strengths and weaknesses are if you can't see them for yourself". He added that he was surprised how many large companies forgot to do this.

I would add that those questions to staff and customers should not be in the form of a survey. Talk to them. One view may not be an answer, but if you start to get the same answers from different people, then consider that they may well be right.

Why is there a gap?

Who has tried before? If you are considering starting a magazine in a field in which nothing exists, then, unless it is an entirely new field of technology, ask why there is a gap. Will those with an interest actually buy a magazine, and, even more important, are there potential advertisers wanting to sell to those people? Check very carefully if there have been previous attempts and whether other publishers have investigated the field. Advertising agencies and the longer established businesses in such fields will have people who will know as may any clubs or associations whose members have an interest in that field. If previous attempts have failed, it does not mean you should not go ahead, but it does mean you must make sure you do not make the same mistakes.

If you are starting a regional magazine, check carefully if that region regards itself as a community. What do the different parts of it have in common?

Chapter 2

The Editor's desk

What is copy?

The material gathered to fill a publication is known among journalists as copy. Much copy is now produced in electronic form, which saves on one of the greatest expenses of publishing — typesetting. But there are many points to consider in specifying the format for receiving copy.

Regardless of the method, you will need to have a clear idea of what sort of content you want, which means clearly working out who your readers are and the kind of stories they want to read. The words story and article are interchangeable in this kind of use — the word 'story' does not carry the implication of being fictional or 'made up' that it does to the general public.

If you want a magazine of short, snappy items, you will not want to receive a treatise of several thousand words. So set out the kind of articles you want and the number of words. If you are running a club magazine then ask for, say, 200 words on what happened on the club's last social outing, to be written so that it will be understood and enjoyed by members who did not go (meaning that it must not have too many in-jokes and disguised references to strange things that happened to individuals).

If it is for a company's house magazine and is a description of a new process, suggest that the author writes it so his or her spouse can understand it.

Ask contributors to prepare their copy in a format that will suit you, but be reasonable.

Receiving the copy

Set out what you want

The most common ways to receive copy are by e-mail and on disk, the most common format now being on CD. Whatever way you prefer, it will pay to set out what you want and in what formats, and put these in a file, perhaps a PDF (portable document format) file which you can send to contributors, or as a web page made available on your web site. If you can expect copy to be submitted on disks, it is reasonable to expect these to be on PC format disks as Macs can read and write PC-formatted disks but not all PCs can read those formatted for the Mac.

There are however a number of computer programs at little or no cost which can enable a Windows-based computer to read a Mac floppy disk or CD.

It is also reasonable to ask for the copy in "text" or "ASCII" format. This means that there will be nothing but alphabetical and numerical information and punctuation marks in the file, plus a few characters like carriage returns. You lose all formatting like bold and italic. All word processing programs have "text" as a "save as" or "export" option. You may also decide that you will accept files in common word processor formats, such as Microsoft Word, though this could lead to you having to buy the latest version as soon as it comes out because one or more of your contributors is sure to do so.

Receiving copy by e-mail opens a whole new can of worms unless you stick to a strict definition of what is acceptable. Straight text in an e-mail message is the simplest means as then you only need a way of stripping out unnecessary carriage returns and odd spacing, which most word processors can do (if you read the manual). Text, Word and other files can also be sent as e-mail attachments. Graphics files can also travel as attachments; make it very clear to your correspondents, however, that graphics cannot be accepted as part of word processing documents. Graphics embedded in word processing documents cause major problems.

Getting at the text

Major word processors will open files prepared in their main competitors. However, they may be at least one version behind. Similarly layout programs will have import filters for files in many different formats and some will also export files in several formats. Some word processors will also have an ability to find text in any file — Microsoft Word has an import option titled "recover text from any file".

Before you spend large amounts on programs, investigate public domain and shareware arenas and the commercial file conversion programs.

Demand a print-out to accompany any disk or if the copy sent by e-mail includes any tables or anything else which needs special formatting, ask for a PDF of the file to accompany the text file, or for a formatted printout to be faxed to you. This "hard copy" will help you gain a quick overall picture of an article and will help if there is difficulty reading the disk. Maybe you will decide from the hard copy that it is not worth going to the trouble of reading a problem disk. A printout is especially useful if there are tables, as sometimes it can be difficult to work out what figures should be in which column.

More about preparing copy — page 129

As a last resort, you could also scan the article and use OCR (optical character recognition) software to convert it to a text file. You need to check the result very carefully, especially names and figures which will not be found in a spellcheck program.

Editorial guidelines

It is common for publications to issue editorial guidelines for contributors, and these often are included on the publication's web site.

Below we include a possible list of editorial guidelines which are intended as a starting point for your consideration. Some you will want to change, and others may be deleted.

Example guidelines

While *The Wellington* has many regular contributors, we are always looking for fresh ideas on the topics listed below. However we do ask you to read a current issue of the magazine before contacting us. In particular, we plan most contents from six to 12 months ahead, so do not send us a proposal for an article about the coming season unless you are clearly indicating something for next year.

We do not accept unsolicited manuscripts. Please send queries only. E-mail is the best way to approach us.

Main features: 1500-2000 word article tied to a current event or issue related to our field. The main story should be accompanied by a separate item of contacts including web addresses.

Tips: 300 words about one aspect of something in our field of interest. Check a current issue for the format.

Profile: Question-and-answer format about a person involved in our field, from 400 to 1000 words with two accompanying photos, one a close-up portrait and the other of the person engaged in their activity.

Briefs: Pieces run from 100-350 words and can be about a person, a region, use of a product, etc.

Regional surveys: Always handled by commission with a general introduction plus items about advertisers associated with the feature. Intro is 300 words plus 100 to 200 words on each business or individual plus a photograph of each.

Humor: 500 to 700 words. Submit previously published items and suggested subjects so that we can see whether your idea of humor is the same as ours.

Book Reviews: Only by arrangement with existing contributors.

Queries should be short and to the point, no longer than one page. First queries should be by mail, with SASE and should include copies of published items. Do not send originals.

We also accept queries by e-mail but first queries should be by mail.

Commissions will be confirmed detailing subject matter, word count, deadline, and payment rate. Submissions should be sent electronically as text files or Word document (.doc) attachments (RTF files acceptable) or on a CD in PC or Mac format. Always send a hard copy of the item as well (though a PDF is also acceptable with electronic submissions). No material will be returned so do not send anything of which you do not keep the original.

A single paragraph biography of the writer(s) should be included at the end of the article.

Writing style: Most articles should be in the present tense with very limited use of first person, in a conversational style. Do not tell the story in the first paragraph (i.e. NOT newspaper style). Define all abbreviations and acronyms on first reference.

Photos: color transparencies or TIFF at 300 dpi to minimum 4" x 6" size (high definition JPEG files are acceptable but should not be enhanced or sharpened in any way — use only the highest quality output from a digital camera with no further compression or enhancement). If a contribution must be compressed it should be in Stuffit or Zip format. A text file should accompany the pictures with captions and file names. Any images in slide or transparency form should also be clearly labeled on the slide case or film to indicate figure number, author and correct orientation. The photographer should obtain a signed model release for any photos including people not the agreed subject of the article, especially for any children, in which case this must be signed by a parent or guardian.

The absolute copy deadline is the first week of the month prior to publication and that will only be by special arrangement for items involving coverage of events. Normal deadlines are eight weeks prior to publication date.

We will not publish material in the same style and format as has appeared in other publications, and never within 6 months of appearance elsewhere. Similarly, we require a 6-month window of use before an item is published elsewhere.

Payment: 30 days after publication. If an article does not appear within three months of the forecast publication date and special arrangements have not been negotiated then a kill fee of 50 per cent of the agreed fee will be paid and all rights will revert to the author.

Expenses will not normally be paid and will only be paid if special arrangements have been agreed in advance. Contra arrangement for any expenses must not be entered into without our knowledge and approval.

Getting illustrations

More on getting at photos — see page 88

It is vital to ask for all illustrations to be sent separately from the text file, though they can also be received as computer files. We will describe ways of getting illustrations out of word processor documents in our chapter on illustrations — suffice it to say here that it is not always easy and even when it works well it takes valuable time.

Word counts

Print samples of type set in columns

All common word processing programs do a word count, but you may like to try a comparison test of the program's number and a manual count to see if you view things the same way.

It is a good idea, even before you start planning the layout of a new publication, to run some copy into column widths and type sizes on your page layout program and then count the words to see just what will fit into a given space in a given type size. Whatever system you use, you will find that there will be times when you have to find other items to fill a page that you have underestimated or cut copy on a page that is too full. As you become more experienced, your estimates of word counts will gradually become more accurate.

If you do not want to have fillers, small stories to fill empty spaces you may need to be more insistent on accurate word counts. It is possible to change type sizes and to adjust interline spacing (leading) to make text fit, but if you do this without a clear plan and design in mind, you may find that you have some very strange looking pages.

Sample setting — page 30 Making stories fit — Chapter 11

As you work your way through this book you will learn some of the devices that can be used to squeeze a little more in or to space out copy that is short.

Preparing a dummy

To plan a magazine, editors typically make up a rough dummy. This can be to actual size or in miniature. Collect a quarter of the number of sheets of paper as there are to be pages in the issue, fold them in half and staple them like the magazine. (If you don't have a long-reach stapler, open out a normal office stapler and put an eraser under the paper. Punch the staple through, then close the staple with a metal rule or a wide-bladed screwdriver.

Now you can number the pages, and write on each page what is to be on that page. Put in the regular things first — for example the contents page, the editorial, any specially placed advertisements, the letters page, and so on. Work in pencil so you can easily move things around.

If you rub out a feature, write it down so it is not left out

But if you rub out a feature and do not immediately place it somewhere else, be sure to write it back on to your list of unused items so that nothing is left out. And obvious things *can* get left out. I have worked on newspapers where some very good front page layouts were produced which then have to be adapted because there was no room allowed for the newspaper masthead. A national magazine once had to take on extra staff to answer angry telephone calls when they left out the crossword.

You can pencil in ideas for layouts, including headlines and use the dummy to get an idea of what illustrations you can use and where they will go. In the early stages of becoming accustomed to this, you will find it better to use a full-size dummy, but later on you may find that a quarter-size one will do.

A listing of pages

Instead of a folded dummy, you may like to use a listing of pages organized so that pages that will appear on the same printed sheet are facing each other on the listing. Figure 2-1 shows an example for a 16-page magazine. The heavier lines show that the four pages in each section are on a single sheet of paper in the finished magazine.

1	16
2	15
3	14
4	13
5	12
6	11
7	10
8	9

Fig.2-1: Such a listing of pages can be a useful guide for allocating space. The heavier line shows that the four pages in each group are on the same single sheet of paper in the finished magazine — in this case a 16-page publication.

Your printer will tell you how to work out which sheets are printed together, and therefore where you can make use of any color that you have at minimum extra cost. Again there will be more on this later.

As you pencil in articles that you have and others that you have asked people to write or which people have told you are coming, so your dummy will fill up.

If someone else is selling advertisements, they will be pencilled in or inked in for those which have to go in specific places.

The flat plan

See also page 126

A third method of planning an issue is the "flat plan", a very rough version of which is shown in Chapter 12 (Figure 12-1). This can sometimes be quite detailed, you can even prepare templates for such plans, based on different combinations of page numbers, to be printed from the office word processor or page layout program.

In the more formal versions, content is indicated on the plan with colored markers used to show ads, features, color availability and much more. It can even take the form of a wall chart.

On the larger publications, this dummy is prepared by the advertisement department who have first call on space (remember, ads pay for the publication!), and given to the editor. On some, the pages may be produced individually and only a running sheet like that shown in Figure 2-1 kept by each department to track pages as they are dealt with and go to the printer.

As you fill the dummy, so you will probably find that some articles are put aside for a later issue, providing an essential stock for when things go wrong and something that was due fails to arrive.

You cannot delay the production to wait for someone who has ignored the deadline. You have to maintain the goodwill of the printer by having the publication with them when you say you will or you will put them off their schedule and the production time gets longer and longer.

Always allow some time for working on the copy so the deadline you set for the author should be at least a day or two before it has to leave you.

Style

Is it all right or alright?

Many publications have style manuals extending to many tens of pages, setting out whether the word is colour or color, whether people are to be called by their full name, with or without the honorific Mr, Mrs, Miss or Ms in front, and whether just first names may be used.

Style manuals will specify whether alright is allowed or whether the wording is all right, whether telephone is preferred to phone or if it has to be 'phone, and if they deal with enquiries or inquiries.

Publications where one person handles all copy can carry on without such niceties. The editor can decide and maybe allow individual writers to have their own variations.

You may find it convenient to adopt the spelling style of your own word processing program, but this is really making man fit the machine instead of vice-versa.

On our web site (or is that website?) you will find a free download of a style guide in various word processor formats ready for you to change as you see fit so it becomes *your* style guide.

Type sizes and fonts

If you are going to do all your own layout work, then everything can be done on the computer, but it may be convenient to settle on a system of marking-up copy. Type sizes and heading styles can be marked on the hard copy before it is given to the computer operator along with the disk. On the other hand, if the copy is prepared on screen, you can insert the type codes which will be read in by the page layout program.

The main requirement is that copy should be clear, without excessive corrections, and with clear instructions for type sizes and styles.

Printing measurements date back to the middle ages and have hardly changed even with the introduction of fully electronic systems. They are universal, applying regardless of the system used for other measurements.

Type sizes are measured in points, and a few examples of common sizes are given on the following page.

The standard sizes are 6, 7, 8, 9, 10, 11, 12, 14, 18, 24, 30, 36, 42, 48, 60 and 72 points. These are shown here in Garamond in Figure 2-2. Most typesetting systems now allow setting in any point size, or even in fractions

Eg Eg Eg Eg Eg Eg Eg Eg Eg Eg

Eg Eg Eg Eg

Fig.2-2: Some of the most common type sizes: 6, 7, 8, 10, 12, 14, 18, 24, 30, 36, 42, 48, 60 and 72pt in a Garamond type face.

of a point. However, the sizes shown are still the most common sizes. Figure 2-3 shows examples of 24 point type in various styles and weights.

Letter spacing, kerning, tracking

Closer as they get bigger

Another way of differentiating in type is letter spacing. It is generally agreed that the spacing between characters decreases slightly as the size increases. When type was made in metal, larger type was made so that it fitted more closely than smaller type and some typesetting systems have retained this ability. However, many systems in common use at present provide only very rudimentary automatic controls for this which means

Times new roman, **bold,** *ital,* ***bold it.***

Helvetica, **bold,** *ital.,* ***bold italic***

Bookman, **bold,** *ital,* ***bold it.***

Palatino, **bold,** *italic,* ***bold italic***

Schoolbook, **bold,** *ital,* ***bold it.***

Zapf Chancery

Fig.2-3: Examples of some common type faces in 24pt size. All these faces are resident in most laser printers.

that closer spacing may need to be specified when styles are set up for headings.

Figure 2-4 on the previous page shows the effects of a general change in letter spacing, or tracking as it is often called, and also the individual spacing between pairs of letters. The latter, called kerning, is used to correct visual imbalance. Most good quality fonts have kerning scales built in and this is probably the main difference between these and cheap fonts available by the thousand on CD. But, even so, you need to look for the worst cases and do something about those: the letters A and V, and W and A are often among the worst.

Take the word WAVE in Fig. 2-4 for example. While spacing in the second case appears more even, in fact the W and A, and A and V are now overlapping.

The more advanced layout systems now take this into account, but it requires a great deal more processing from the computers.

Type faces for body text

Look at any catalogue of type faces and you will see that faces can be condensed, regular or expanded, and light, regular, bold and even extra bold. Some may also have semibold. However, not all typesetting systems can do all things. Print out, or get printed out, a selection of typesetting in every style and weight, making sure that you include letters with ascenders and descenders; ascenders are the upper' parts of letters like 'b' and 'd' while descenders are the 'tails' of letters such as 'g' and 'p'.

You will notice that some type faces of the same size appear to be quite different.

One face: different tracking
One face: different tracking

WAVE

WAVE

Fig.2-4: Letter spacing or tracking can be generally looser or tighter and individual letter spacing, called kerning, helps appearance.,

Examples of body text typesetting:

There are many thousands of type faces but they fall into a number of groups. The main ones are serif and sans-serif faces, the latter usually called sans for short (sans is French for without, i.e. without serifs). Serifs are the little extensions at the extremities of letters and examples are clearly seen in the samples. There are many thousands of type faces but they fall into a number of groups. The main ones are serif and sans-serif faces, the latter usually called sans for short (sans is French for without, i.e. without serifs). Serifs are the little extensions at the extremities of letters and examples are clearly

8pt Times 8pt leading

There are many thousands of type faces but they fall into a number of groups. The main ones are serif and sans-serif faces, the latter usually called sans for short (sans is French for without, i.e. without serifs). Serifs are the little extensions at the extremities of letters and examples are clearly seen in the samples. There are many thousands of type faces but they fall into a number of

10pt Times 10pt leading

There are many thousands of type faces but they fall into a number of groups. The main ones are serif and sans-serif faces, the latter usually called sans for short (sans is French for without, i.e. without serifs). Serifs are the little extensions at the extremities of letters and examples are clearly seen in the samples. There are many thousands of type faces but they fall into a number of groups.

9pt Helvetica 10pt leading

There are many thousands of type faces but they fall into a number of groups. The main ones are serif and sans-serif faces, the latter usually called sans for short (sans is French for without, i.e. without serifs). Serifs are the little extensions at the extremities of letters and examples are clearly seen in the samples. There are many thousands of type faces but they fall into a number of groups. The main ones are serif and sans-serif faces, the latter usually called sans for short (sans is French for without, i.e. without serifs). Serifs are the

8pt Times 9pt leading

There are many thousands of type faces but they fall into a number of groups. The main ones are serif and sans-serif faces, the latter usually called sans for short (sans is French for without, i.e. without serifs). Serifs are the little extensions at the extremities of letters and examples are clearly seen in the samples. There

10pt Times 12pt leading

There are many thousands of type faces but they fall into a number of groups. The main ones are serif and sans-serif faces, the latter usually called sans for short (sans is French for without, i.e. without serifs). Serifs are the little extensions at the extremities of letters and examples are clearly seen in the samples. There are many thousands of type faces but they fall into a number of groups. The main ones are serif and sans-serif faces, the latter usually called sans for short (sans is French for without, i.e. without serifs). Serifs

9pt Helvetica narrow 9pt leading

There are many thousands of type faces but they fall into a number of groups. The main ones are serif and sans-serif faces, the latter usually called sans for short (sans is French for without, i.e. without serifs). Serifs are the little extensions at the extremities of letters and examples are clearly seen in the samples. There are many thousands of type faces but they fall into a number of groups. The main ones are serif and sans-serif faces, the latter usually called sans for short (sans

9pt Times 9pt leading

There are many thousands of type faces but they fall into a number of groups. The main ones are serif and sans-serif faces, the latter usually called sans for short (sans is French for without, i.e. without serifs). Serifs are the little extensions at the extremities of letters and examples are clearly seen in the samples. There are many thousands of type faces but they fall into a number of groups. The main ones are serif and sans-serif faces.

9pt Helvetica 9pt leading

There are many thousands of type faces but they fall into a number of groups. The main ones are serif and sans-serif faces, the latter usually called sans for short (sans is French for without, i.e. without serifs). Serifs are the little extensions at the extremities of letters and examples are clearly

10pt Helvetica 12pt leading

Fig.2-5: Examples of body type in two of the most common types: Times and Helvetica.

This is because they are based on the old days of metal type, when the measurement was of the physical size of the metal rather than the type image.

However, the number of lines of 10 pt type to a given depth will always be the same, whatever the type face.

Ems, picas and other strange measurements

There are 12 points to a pica em, commonly called either a pica (pronounced piker) or an em, though strictly speaking an em is a measure of width based on the height of the type size involved, so an 8 pt em is in fact 8 points wide. But this is just adding confusion. For general purposes an em or a pica is a width equal to 12 points. Half an em is an en (6 pt).

More on advertisement sizes — see page 43

Your column and page widths and depths may be given in inches, centimetres or picas, and it is quite possible for individual staff members to operate their own way. You do not have to change once you have established which way you find most convenient. As advertisements are now most commonly measured in centimetres of depth in Europe and inches in the USA, it will probably lead to least confusion if the appropriate measure for your area is used for all measurements of depth.

I have included on the previous page some examples of type set in a variety of sizes, styles and column width, along with the number of words in each sample.

You will see that as well as type size, the type face can make quite a difference to the space any given copy will take up. This is because type width can vary considerably — compare the standard and narrow versions of Helvetica on the previous page.

There are many thousands of type faces, but they fall into a number of groups.

The main ones are serif and sans-serif faces, the latter usually called sans for short (sans is French for without). Serifs are the little extensions at the extremities of letters and examples are clearly seen in the samples printed in this chapter. The shapes of serifs can vary, and a large sub-section of the serif kind is called slab-serif, with very square-looking serifs.

Perhaps the best-known of all types is that designed originally for *The Times* newspaper of London, and given the name Times New Roman. It has been replaced twice since then, with Times Europa in the 1970s and with Times Millennium at the end of the century, a font designed for modern printing. Ink used to spread noticeably when metal type was pressed into absorbent paper such as newsprint so fonts were designed to take this into account; now this effect is much less noticeable.

Most typesetting systems offer either Times or something that is a copy

Arial or Helvetica?

of it, and similarly they will offer either the most common of sans types, Helvetica, or something very like it. The Arial type face, which comes with the Windows operating system, is similar to Helvetica and identical in spacing though not in design.

Here's an example of a couple of characters in Helvetica on the left and Arial on the right:

abtGR   abtGR

Did you notice the tail on the 'a', the slope of the top on the 't', the spur on the 'G' and the slope on the leg of the 'R'?

Your type style will be largely set by what your computer and printer can offer, but it will almost certainly have a variety of both serif and sans types.

More about imagesetters — page 60

There are other considerations. For example, if you will be printing your pages out on a laser printer or an imagesetter (we'll go into what that is later on), there will be a selection of built-in fonts. If you use these not only will your print files be smaller but the time taken to print each page will be less, although as computer power has increased, this consideration has become less important. In fact, now, it may be better to opt for settings which deliberately download all fonts from the computer to ensure you print exactly the version of a font that you have used in the layout program. Newer fonts may include characters which are not in older versions of those fonts which may be built into older laser printers (the Euro symbol, €, is an example).

The type face is part of the design of your publication, and you should consider whether the type face is right for the job you want it to do. For example, although I have mentioned that Times is one of the most common faces, this was a type face designed for a newspaper printed on high quality newsprint. It tends therefore to fill in on poorer quality paper

Brioso Pro Light, Regular, Medium, **Semibold, Bold** and *Italic Light, Regular, Medium, Semibold, Bold* with variations for use at a range of sizes from caption to poster with a Range of Swash and alternate letters.

Fig.2-6: As might be expected with so much variety in one family of types, Adobe's Brioso Pro OpenType font comes with a multipage PDF on how to drive it.

and to be somewhat spidery on coated paper. There are other type faces more suited to both these extremes.

Paragraph styles

Set up your tags

If you are typesetting your own publication, you can set up "styles" or "tags" in any word processing or page layout program. This enables the person doing the typesetting, or preparing a file for print, to specify, for example "body text" and have the style you have specified in advance applied automatically. However, if you use a variety of typesetting styles and do not apply them yourself, you will need a means of "marking up" the copy. Rather than give the type size, the style, and the width you want it set, it is much easier to specify "mymag body" — a style which can be created to incorporate all these attributes.

More about style tags — pages 129 and 148

As the column width can be easily changed in the layout program, you may dispense with this specification and have everything set to a standard measure for initial proofing. Headings and intros (which is what we generally call introductory paragraphs for short) may have to be specified at this stage but it is also now more common to have everything typeset and proofed in a standard size and style.

More about layout — see Chapter 11, page 105

You will find many type faces that are similar but with different names. Sometimes this may be to avoid paying royalties to the original type designer but equally it may be because several faces are based on the same original type design. You will also find some confusion over the use of the terms face and font (font is the technical term for the main subdivision of a type face).

For most uses, one family of types for headings with perhaps another used occasionally for contrast, and a single family for the body matter with

Fig.2-7: In a simple text editor, this is an example of simple text tags (which can be used just as easily in a full word processor such as Microsoft Word. The tags in this case <head>, <first par> and <Body text>, tell the layout program when the text is imported to apply those styles.

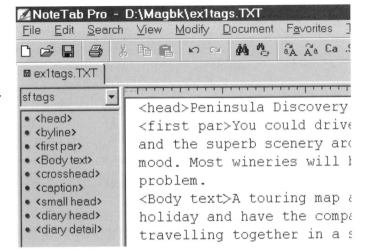

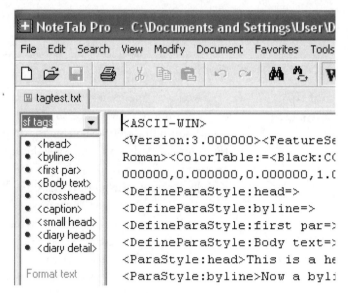

Fig.2-8: These are tags as used by InDesign and seen in the same text editor as Fig.2-7. They are similar to those used by PageMaker and QuarkXPress but not quite interchangeable. In this system you define the styles, but if they already exist in the template you do not have to detail what they are in the text file. There is also an abbreviated way of defining each command which is ideal for database output.

maybe a contrasting type for some special features, is enough. You need the special skills of a typographer to be able to mix types at will without creating a hotchpotch of confusion. And the skilled typographer is more likely to produce a great variety of pages with a relatively small selection of fonts.

The best way of learning about magazine layout is to look at lots of magazines, deciding what you like and then trying to see why it has worked and exactly how any special effects were achieved.

Legibility

Who will read it?

One aspect of typesetting which applies equally to editorial and advertisements but which we will deal with here is the question of readability.

This involves much more than just the choice of type size and face and for example you would also take into consideration the readership for which your publication is intended.

Sight deteriorates with age and so in very basic terms one would expect a publication to be in larger, clearer type for older readers. It is noticeable that magazines intended for a teenage readership make much greater use of layout "tricks" such as reversed text and text overlaid on tints and of use of one color for text on a colored background. Such items are much easier to decipher with younger eyes. Very young children do need very simple type setting.

You'll read in various reports you'll find on the Web that text for over-60s should be in Arial font, at 14 pt, with no italics and a preference for bold — but that's for readers who are "vision impaired", not your normal "senior citizen".

Type & Layout

Lots of people have opinions on these matters, but none can beat the research of Colin Wheildon in Sydney, Australia. The work was initially published by the Newspaper Advertising Bureau in Australia, then by Strathmoor Press in California under the title *Type & Layout: How Typography and Design Can Get Your Message Across – or Get In the Way* and is soon to be reissued in a new and updated edition by Worsley Press (Keep an eye on our web site). This is the source of the general view that serif type is more readable for the general reader and that other factors such as contrast and line length relative to point size and leading can be more important than just point size.

A publishing timetable

Plan ahead

As the editor of a magazine or newsletter you will have to plan ahead and the larger a publication gets the more you will have to set a detailed timetable, with different schedules for the content of various sections.

With many magazines, the news section for the issue which will hit the newsstands in a month's time may be closing now, but the feature sections will have been ready to go at least one month earlier. That's finalized, proofed pages.

Decisions on what will go in those pages could well be taken three months ahead — but of course if events take over, features without a news hook will be moved back one or more issues.

Decisions on changes in regular content are probably made on certain dates — perhaps with the season, so if you miss one, and are still in the running, it could well be six months.

The most confusing magazine I've worked for was Australia's leading TV guide during the days when there were a lot of independent and semi-independent regional stations — there were always at least 10 editions of the magazine, all with internal editorial changes to reflect programs in the area, but also the time it would take to freight copies to the region, meaning that there were always five different week's issues actually in production at any time involving several different regional editions of each. At one stage I was laying out and editing the double page spread of movies on this week (which week? which area?) at the rate of three or four spreads a day.

Illusion of being up to date

Few other magazines have those complications but it is common for things to be considered like special local advertising and what page space may be in different editions. Large magazines tend to be a little like oil tankers — the captain makes a decision to change direction and something happens several months later. That they seem current and occasionally report events which seem to have happened only a few days earlier is more illusion than reality.

This does cause confusion, especially for neophyte contributors who may well believe that because the items of the day's newspaper which they receive at breakfast contains news said to have been written at 2am that the whole of the paper is finalized at that time. They appreciate that a monthly magazine takes a little longer, but not that it has to be planned months ahead. You may need to point this out to your contributors.

Exclusive use of editorial

Tell your writers…

You also need to make it clear to contributors whether what they write for you is to be exclusive or whether it can be submitted elsewhere.

I recently answered a question from a writer for a magazine on just this point. I suggested that a local magazine's submission conditions were pretty normal: that the writer not submit anything similar to any other local publication for six months after the date submitted to them and not to submit anything which might have been published locally in the previous six months.

The decision on whether it is reasonable to ask for it not to be submitted elsewhere would usually be: "Can it be expected that someone reading their publication will see the other publication in which it may appear?"

So if this is a country/rural magazine near two urban areas, my interpretation would be that it is a reasonable request. It is obviously not reasonable for a country magazine in California to ask that a writer not let it be published in New York, even if they have a couple of dozen subscribers in New York or the NY magazine sells a few copies in the Californian magazine's circulation area.

The decision also depends a lot on whether the writer is getting paid, and if so, how much. If it is basically a press release but the writer is going to get special treatment in your publication in return for not submitting the same article elsewhere, then it depends what the advantage will be to both publisher and writer.

My reaction as an editor would probably be that I'd ask the writer to give us an exclusive in our distribution area and I'd ask for but not necessarily expect to get it exclusive in adjacent areas. I'd also accept that if we are not paying for it, that the writer would be within his or her rights to offer the same information but in a different form to other publications.

The six months requested here also seemed reasonable based on the other conditions. I would have asked for a year.

What do you call an editor?

Many titles for a few jobs

Not long before starting work on this edition, we answered an e-mail from someone who was preparing a newsletter for a company and who did not have the final say in what appeared, since alterations would be made even after she had seen page proofs. She was listed as editor in the publication and was concerned that she was not really getting paid for that work. Our advice was to immediately ask to have her name removed, even if it was retained as a contact for editorial in the newsletter. Being listed as editor means taking responsibility for all that appears and obviously in this publication she did not have authority to make final decisions.

There are many degrees of editorship, and there are no clear definitions of terms such as Publisher, Editor, Managing Editor, Editorial Director, Editor in Chief, Group Editor, and many more.

Where the editor on one magazine may be the senior person who makes final decisions on content and layout, and has input into the financial side, the same term on another magazine could describe the third or fourth in line who has little say on anything other than the content of individual articles.

You will find that the Director of Advertising will usually be in charge of the ad sales department, but that could be the Advertisement Manager or the Advertising Manager (my argument is that the Advertising Manager is someone who works for an advertiser and controls the advertising they place, whereas on a publication the term refers to the person who manages the incoming advertisements and so should be Advertisement Manager).

Publisher may refer to someone who is the overall boss, but it could mean the person who looks after the management of everything but perhaps not the editorial. At least it does not have as wide a meaning as in newspapers where it could mean the person who owns the newspaper chain, or the junior person who makes sure the editions get from the press to the delivery trucks on schedule.

More on legal aspects — Chapter 18, page 179

All this information together with contact details, any statement of legal liabilities, responsibilities for election comment in states where that is necessary, printer's name and any copyright information, all goes in a box with the upmarket term of the colophon. I have also heard it colloquially called the "skite box".

On larger publications the position of publisher may be filled from any of the departments under his or her control, but it tends to usually be from what is seen as the 'business' side, advertising, or from the production side, seldom from editorial and almost never from circulation.

Finding editorial

Ideas aplenty

A question often asked of editors is "where do you find the ideas for articles?" I recall the answer to that question by the editor of a major women's magazine regarding where the idea came for one of the main features that week. Her answer: "I found it hidden away on the front page of the morning newspaper."

There is an impression that it is a constant search for new ideas, whereas the task should be one of selecting the best. Notes should be made of ideas as they come up, and on larger publications there are likely to be editorial meetings where far more ideas are produced than can ever be followed. Many ideas will be for series of articles, even if they are not presented as such; for example, interviews with people involved in the field the publication covers. Also, while a magazine cannot present news as such, there will always be a diary of events about which items will be written well in advance.

Newspapers will always be a source of ideas, as the editor of the women's magazine said, but usually by following up one aspect of a news item as it might affect the magazine's readers. Then there are reader's letters; any questions they pose could well be worth considering, even if the reader would never guess that an article which appears many months later was prompted by his or her comment.

Watching others

Other magazines and newsletters should also be watched carefully. We have seen comments about how an idea for a new regular feature in one will soon be followed by similar features in others, but no editor can afford to ignore an area of interest which might cause readers to switch loyalties. However, there will also be ideas dealt with lightly by the opposition which the editor feels could be considered at greater depth.

Chapter 3

Advertisements

Most of the income
Whenever a free publication is poked in a letterbox, it seems that someone is bound to ask "But how do they make it pay?"

It is an unfortunate fact of publishing life that most publications make most of their income from advertisements, and while that becomes especially noticeable with free publications, it somehow remains hidden for most people in others — even if the little they pay for a massive weekend newspaper would not buy a scrap pad of a fraction that size at the same newsstand.

This is particularly unfortunate for small publications which do not have a big appeal to advertisers as it makes the cover price seem excessively expensive by comparison.

So a first major consideration you have to make with a new magazine or newsletter is whether you will take advertisements, and the extent to which there will be a demand for space from advertisers. You also have to decide what proportion of costs you intend (or hope) to cover from advertisements.

Let us start simply. You currently have the meeting reminder notice that we mentioned in an earlier chapter, and propose turning this into a monthly newsletter.

Your present costs are for paper and postage — with photocopying time and typing donated. As a magazine it will initially have similar costs,

Using PDFs
You may decide to have a printed cover, carrying advertisements, and in the previous editions of this book we have suggested you consider getting quotes for printing these in sufficient quantities for six or 12 months.

Now we would suggest getting the ads set professionally if you aren't sure you can do them to a sufficient standard yourself, and for these to be supplied as PDF files either for the complete sheet or pages. You can then either print them on your own printer as needed from the free Adobe Reader program (formerly known as Acrobat Reader) or you can incorporate the PDF files into the word processing or page layout program you are using for your editorial pages.

The complete file can then be saved as a PDF and taken to a copyshop or print centre if the required number is too many to print out yourself.

One warning: it is normally not a problem to include a PDF within a file that will be itself made into a PDF, but there are limits to the number of iterations so if the original PDF includes graphics which are themselves in PDF or EPS format, and you then ask your printer to print groups of pages (which he could do by putting PDFs together) you could reach that limit. Don't worry with small publication jobs but do be aware that if you do hit a problem, this just might be the cause.

You may be surprised at how little extra it costs to print a larger number of covers, perhaps sufficient for several issues, and plan to overprint the date or issue number on a laser printer or photocopier, but consider how likely it is that an advertiser may move or change their web site or e-mail address which could mean scrapping the lot.

On the other hand it is possible to make small changes in a PDF using the full Acrobat program (not just the free Reader), or in a word processor or layout program you can always do the equivalent of a paste-up correction: place a filled box over the error and type in the new material.

Think of some rates

If you decide that you will have advertisements on three of the four cover pages then two of them may be divided into halves and the other into quarters (or any other combination you think you can sell). You can divide the total cost you wish to cover (let us say $400) by three pages, to give $134 a page, and by halves and quarters to give $62 a half page and $31 a quarter.

Now depending on your potential advertisers, that may sound very little, or it may seem a lot, even for a year's advertising. But it is the minimum, or else you will not be paying for the cost of the extra cover.

You may decide that the rates should be $300 a page, $160 a half and $85 a quarter. I have plucked these figures out of the air, and I suggest that as a starting point you do the same, to see how they look as value for money in terms of what the advertiser will get and in what income you may need.

If you have been given (or have calculated) a separate typesetting cost for the advertisements, as you may be for a more substantial printing order on a complete magazine, you may like to base the rates on the actual space as a proportion of the total revenue needed, plus the actual typesetting cost for each space, rounded to the nearest dollar or 50 cents.

Spreadsheet for 'what if' calculations

Download this file — see page 4

This is what we have done to produce the advertisement rates and revenue spreadsheet which you can download from our web site. This is shown in Fig.3-1 and allows for a wide range of "what if" calculations.

In the example shown here we have a 16-page magazine and have decided that we should aim for a quarter of that to be advertisements (not

MAGAZINE OR NEWSLETTER AD RATE AND INCOME CALCULATOR

(Cells that can be changed are shown in Blue: use Tab key to move through them)

The things we need to know:

No of pages in typical issue:		16
Maximum percentage of ad pages:		25%
Full page suggested rate:		$500
Extra % for smaller ads:		5%
Discount % per series step:		10%
Weekly or monthly (W/M):		M
Approx % at repeats for series of:	3	20%
	6	20%
	12	30%

Any of the items in blue can be changed and these changes will be reflected in the rest of the spreadsheet. Most are self explanatory but the percentage entry for smaller ads is the jump in price at each level, e.g. a 10% jump will mean that where a full page costs $100, a half page costs half that plus 10% ($55) and similarly a percentage reduction would apply for each series step.

Your rate card could look like this:

No of insertions:	1	3	6	12
Full page:	$500.00	$450.00	$405.00	$365.00
Half page:	$262.50	$236.30	$212.70	$191.70
Quarter page:	$137.90	$124.10	$111.70	$100.70
Eighth page:	$72.40	$65.20	$58.70	$52.90
Sixteenth page:	$38.10	$34.30	$30.90	$27.80

Mix of ads

			Cumulative total	Revenue at full rates:
Total number of ad pages:	4			
Enter various combinations below to see effect on revenue				
No. of full pages:		2	2.00	$1,000.00
No. of half pages:		2	3.00	$525.00
No. of quarter pages:		2	3.50	$275.80
No. of eighth pages:		1	3.63	$72.40
No. of sixteenth pages:		2	3.75	$76.20
				$1,949.40

After calculating for the proportion of repeat ads...

Likely revenue per issue: **$1,656.99**

These are the two areas in which details can be changed. All other figures change as a result of entries in these sections

Fig.3-1: This income and rate calculator is available free on this book's web site. See page 4 for details.

necessarily as four complete pages, but a total equivalent to the space of four pages).

I should give an explanation of three entry items which seem to cause some confusion. The "extra % for smaller ads" is the percentage by which a smaller ad price is more than its proportion of the bigger one; for example if this is set at 5%, a half page will be 5 per cent more than half a full page rate, so if a full page is $500, a half page will be $262.50 (500/2 × 1.05). The discount for a series of ads means, if that is set to 5%, that if a full page is $500, the rate for each ad when a page is taken in each of three issues will be $450 (500 × 0.95).

Because revenue can be reduced quite dramatically if you get more ads at series rates, the spreadsheet lets you enter various percentages of ads that come at series discounts. This allows for some "worst case" calculations, though presumably if you have most ads booked for multiple issues, your costs of selling should be less than if you have to sell each ad one by one.

It will also help if you get a copy of the advertisement rates for any specialist magazines in your field, and of the local newspapers, along with approximate circulation figures. These rates are often given in publications, or can be found from publications' web sites, reference books in your local library, or by telephoning the publications.

See Chapter 16 — page 161

In our chapter on Economics, we will look more closely at the comparison of costs and income but you may well end up with a frightening loss figure unless you set an advertisement rate that is higher than you would like.

Extra revenue increases costs

Editorial costs may rise too

When you calculate the revenue from the number of advertisements you hope to get at the rate you would like to charge for them, don't forget to increase the estimated cost of production by sufficient to cover the printing of those extra pages, and allow also that buyers may not be interested in a magazine that seems to be full of advertisements, so you may have to increase the editorial costs too, or reduce the cover price.

Smaller advertisements generally cost relatively more to typeset, though you may be lucky and get smaller ads from people who are happy to have very simple typesetting — those who take larger spaces are likely also to have increased demands for designs and proofs, and corrections.

If you are lucky, your loss may have turned into a healthy paper profit, but you may have to do a lot of juggling with advertisement rates, relative issue sizes, cover prices and other costs before you find a realistic budget. With a computer and a spreadsheet program you may be able to work out a lot of these "what-if?" questions more easily.

Discount structures

Encourage regular ads

It is normal with advertisements in magazines to offer a discount for numbers of insertions, whereas in newspapers it is usual to base the discount on the total number of column centimetres or inches taken in a year or in a single contract.

The magazine system encourages advertisers to appear in every issue, but can be taken advantage of by advertisers taking a minimum space every month just to gain a big reduction on one or two whole pages. One rate card I saw would allow an advertiser to take a couple of half pages and then 10 small ads for the rest of the year at a total cost of less than taking just two half pages. Make sure that you do not make the same mistake.

You should also look carefully at the rate you get on maximum discount for the largest spaces. If you are lucky enough to gain a large number of ads for every issue, you may find your success marred by the low return on these ads.

Dangers in special offers

A similar problem can occur if you make some specific offers like three ads for the price of two, or four for the price of three. If you charge them the rate for the first insertions you may find that your third or fourth issue brings you very little revenue. If you average the cost over each ad then you may find your return per page drops below an acceptable level. Such offers sound good, and are relatively easy to sell, but they are best reserved for classified ads where they can help increase the return on pages which may sometimes be relatively full of house ads.

Be wary of offering a guarantee of circulation by means of a discount if the circulation of a new publication does not live up to expectations. It is commonly used by large publishers on new titles but most exclude initial issues where there may be an introductory discount already and use it just to get over that hiatus between initial interest and bookings based on proven response and audited figures.

Advertisement sizes

Proportions of a page

So far we have discussed advertisements as proportions of a page as this is the normal way of selling magazine ads: page, half-page, quarter-page, eighth-page, sometimes even sixteenth-page. It may also be likely that spaces are sold by thirds of a page, particularly in publications which have three editorial columns to a page, with one-third and two-thirds vertical and one-sixth which will be half the depth of the one-third of a page. There can also be special sizes for smaller display ads grouped together.

Some publications sell smaller ads by the column inch or in two-centimetre or 20mm units as appropriate and a lesson can also be taken from the yellow pages business telephone directories in several countries which sell by the "unit" with larger display ads being 2-unit or 3-unit and so on. There is also, in the USA, a special unit called the SAU or "standard advertising unit" which is almost exclusive to newspapers but which you may consider if your publication has a newspaper look. The basis of the SAU is 2⅛" wide by 1" deep but there are a wide variety of specific SAU sizes and shapes. Another measure used in newspapers in the USA which occasionally makes its way into magazines is the agate, an ancient print measurement. There are 14 agate lines to an inch.

When you are calculating your ad sizes, don't forget to allow for the space between ads when dividing the total page size into sections and, if you are hoping as a new publication to pick up ads from existing publications it

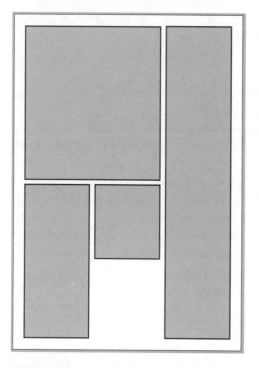

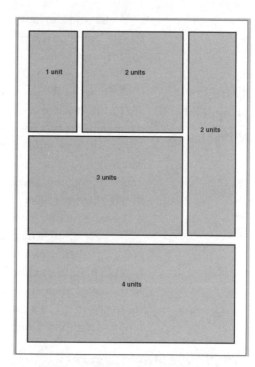

Fig.3-2: Some ad sizes other than the standard ones shown in Fig.1-1 on page 17.

may be worth considering that it will be easier to incorporate ads prepared for use elsewhere if your spaces are fractionally larger, but may present major difficulties if they are a little smaller. Another example is that if you have a larger page size you may consider a specific ad size equivalent to a page in your smaller opposition which may, for example run over three of your four columns and to perhaps three-quarters of your page height.

Advertising agencies

Giving discounts

If most advertisements will be booked through advertising agencies, you will automatically have to deduct 10 or 15 per cent from the overall revenue because agencies derive their income from discounts they get from media. In some cases you will benefit from many of the ads being supplied as complete artwork so you do not have any setting charges, but it is also worthwhile looking at separating the space charge from the typesetting charge for all advertisers. You may also like to consider offering a discount for prompt payment, though weigh against this the likelihood that the prompt payer will be prompt anyway.

Typesetting costs

A very real expense

Typesetting of advertisements is a very real cost to the publisher even though if it is done in your own office rather than being shown on a typesetter's or service bureau's bill. If this work is being contracted out, it should be based on the actual number typeset, especially if you find that a greater number of ads than originally forecast come in as camera-ready artwork or are repeats of standing copy.

You should regularly divide your total bills, or estimates of internal costs, and the subsections of those costs or charges, by the number of pages, so that you have a continuing guide to what each page costs to produce. There will be variations because you cannot increase and decrease the magazine by single pages, but the average of several issues will provide a good guide.

What are you selling?

It's access to readers

Selling advertisement space is like selling any product, except that in this case, the sale is of something rather more ethereal. The customer cannot see what he is buying. Therefore it is even more necessary to sell the benefits rather than the product itself. What you are selling is access to your readership — the opportunity for the advertiser to put their message to your readership. With information on your readership you should know if your advertisers can sell an image or if they should be giving lots of details to readers who will check every detail of specifications — even if they need a magnifying glass to do it.

You need to be well armed with statistics about your readership, and the market in general. But on a very practical basis I have found it an advantage to include in a rate folder (which I prefer to a rate card, as it enables much more promotional material to be included along with the harsh reality of the rates), an empty space equal to the most common advertisement space — a half or quarter page for example. It is surprising how often you will see the client begin to pencil in what he wants to say before verbally committing to the sale.

Discounts cause future problems

The primary error made in selling space is to succumb to the ease of making a sale by offering a discount. Be warned, once you have offered a discount it is very difficult to avoid making a similar offer in future. The seller of space should have plenty of other incentives at hand including timing (the need for the advertiser to reach the market ahead of a new season, or to promote a new product, or even for themselves to offer a discount to clear stock ahead of a new model). There are also the incentives built in to the rate card such as discounts for larger spaces and for committing to a series of ads or to a specific amount of space in a set period, usually a year. In some cases it can be as simple as asking for the order.

There are two situations where discounts should be offered: when a mistake has been made by the publication which is not great enough to give a free insertion, and, very occasionally or it will be seen as a ruse to make a sale, the last minute replacement for an advertiser who has pulled out. In the latter case you will be offering a specific space in a specific place in the publication and will need the copy instructions on the spot, preferably a repeat of an ad you already have.

Be prepared to quote rates in terms of CPM (cost per thousand, using the roman numeral 'M' for 1000). These figures are produced by dividing your ad cost by the circulation or readership. It's a good way of comparing competitive media, even to radio as a cost per thousand listeners. Use it if it works to your advantage.

Selling extras

The other way to increase ad revenue than selling more space is to increase the advertisement value in other ways, such as by selling special positions (back cover, page 3, facing specific editorial features), by selling color (full or spot) and perhaps by selling bleed advertisements where the advertiser gains the margin space. With the latter, be sure that such an ad can be printed in that position as there are some pages which cannot bleed. Bleed ads do not have to be full page; they can be effective as half pages or less horizontally and vertically. A common surcharge for bleed is 20 per cent, but you need to do your sums as some printers will quote by default on a basis of "no bleeds" on inside pages. Surcharges for special positions can be 100 per cent or more — it depends on the demand.

As I mention in our chapter on economics, advance advertisement orders are an asset, even though you may have difficulty persuading a bank to lend you money against them.

Advertisement features and 'advertorial'

Crossing the divide

Will your publication allow a crossing of the divide between advertisements and editorial? This is the "advertorial" which some publications insist should carry the words Advertisement Feature or Advertisement above the text. Such features do not have to be shame-faced plugs for the advertiser; they can, for example, be interesting interviews with the business owner or advice on using a product. However, they do have the effect of reducing advertisement revenue, sometimes to half what it should be for those sections, and the reader will have less faith in the "advertorial" content.

On a publication which has well separated editorial and advertisement departments, writers may regard the writing of accompanying editorial as a chore, and so it becomes an effort to maintain writing standards, even in the face of an item such as a report on an entirely new business which could well be worth similar space in the editorial columns.

Commissions

Guarantee from agents

I have mentioned the established system of sales commissions to agents for advertisements. This should be granted only to recognized agencies, members of the appropriate professional body, where you gain in the form of a guarantee of payment regardless of what happens to the client.

Also, be wary of agents acting as advertisement representatives. There are many reputable firms who offer the services of representatives in cities where the publisher cannot have their own staff. However, there are also a number of doubtful companies.

Agents to sell for you

You also have to work out whether the revenue gives you a profit after deducting the relatively high commission the representative has to charge. It can be 50 per cent or more on new orders, usually reducing considerably for repeat bookings. Could you do as well with a few long-distance telephone calls, a very occasional visit and some mailing shots? Agents may want to take over all advertisements from their area, but it is common for the publisher to reserve existing clients, or those where you have already put in considerable effort as "house clients".

Most publications that use such agents list them for direct contact by potential advertisers. If they represent reputable publications, it is most likely they are reputable themselves, but they may not be able to achieve much for small publications. You will be just one more title on a representative's list, but they may be able to achieve a good return if you have an attractive offer for a substantial special issue and give the agent sufficient advance notice.

Agents overseas

Overseas agents will often welcome the opportunity to add your publication to their lists, and while the revenue that finds it way through to you will be small, you may decide that it is worth the prestige of carrying such advertisements. If they start coming in quantity you may have to renegotiate the terms.

Co-operative advertising

Subsidies for retailers

Many large companies offer a subsidy towards advertisements placed by retailers who stock or are agents for their products or services. Copy is usually supplied by the major company via the retailer with the retailer just adding their contact details. Occasionally the retailer will organise for space used to promote several suppliers to be paid by those suppliers and expect the publisher to invoice them with various percentages of the overall cost. I've occasionally come across a retailer whose percentages total to more than 100 per cent, and who expects the extra to be credited to their account. It is a good way of getting extra ads out of retailers who sell nationally branded products but causes fewest problems if it is entirely run by the retailer with you invoicing as usual and leaving it up to them to collect from the suppliers.

On the other hand it can bring in national advertising, and sometimes works by the national advertiser booking space on a basis that one or more local agents take a small space immediately beneath. In other words, it is worth asking advertisers whether they have access to co-operative advertising — but watch for scams with you as the victim.

Watch also for arrangements by which someone books a large space, such as a full page or spread, and sells it in smaller spaces. This can be effective for shopping centres, retailers associations and other groups, but keep a close watch or you may find that your overall page yield (the total income divided by the total number of ad pages) drops away because you lose in individual sales and have higher typesetting costs for the page.

Classified advertising

You should also consider whether to include a section of classified, or unclassified, small advertisements. With small monthly publications there is not generally a large scope for such advertisements, and in fact, many such magazines include a column or page of such notices without charge as a service to the reader.

The problem is that most small advertisements are for sales of secondhand items, and usually, the seller wants to be able to get the advertisement in and the item sold within a few days, whereas monthly magazine deadlines may mean the delay becomes weeks. However, in a specialist field, the ability to reach that particular market may outweigh the disadvantage of time.

A way of at least partially overcoming this problem is via a web page — ads can be listed as soon as they are received. As you will be charging for the ad as a combined web/print insertion, the full fee is payable even if the advertiser cancels the print appearance because the item is sold. The ad has done its job.

There are a number of regional publications that consist almost exclusively of classified advertisements, often with payment by result. The system depends on a certain amount of honesty, but would-be buyers who find that items were sold some time before, or who see the advertisement appear again after they have been told the item has gone, are encouraged to inform the publisher.

Small advertisements are usually accepted on a cash-with-order basis and, being just run-on copy, cost little to set, so they can be fairly cheap and yet still be profitable. As production runs become longer, so the size of type used in classifieds tends to become smaller to enable the individual ad price to be kept low. To optimize this, much effort has gone into designing types as small as 4¾ point for some newspapers, usually with names such as Adsans.

If you feel there is a good potential market, it may be worth including an order-blank, with a grid in which people can write their advertisement — one word in each box — enabling them to accurately calculate the cost. This form also helps to ensure that classified advertisers include such essential information as their name and address.

If the number of advertisements is likely to be small, it may save you much effort if you run them as "unclassifieds" — readers mostly enjoy hunting through several columns for bargains.

Success breeds success

Classifieds is an area where success breeds success, so, if you can appear to have several pages full of classified advertisements, you may find that you do indeed start to receive bookings. Rather than making it too obvious our classifieds were free in one publication, we photocopied some "special offer" sheets that were given away at selected events. We also sent display advertisers such offers with their invoice. The note invited them to "write your free classified on the back and send this back with your account payment". I think this something-for-nothing offer may have even encouraged some earlier payments.

How copy is submitted

Whose job to set the ads?

Over the years responsibility for the preparation of advertisements has see-sawed between the publication and the advertiser. With hot metal typesetting the words were typeset by the publication which would probably also be responsible for turning any illustrations into what were called printing blocks or photo-engravings.

Then larger advertisers began to prepare (or employ people to prepare) the complete advertisement, submitted as metal plates either engraved individually or prepared by making papier-mâché moulds and pouring in molten typemetal. The responsibility had moved to the advertiser as it was difficult and expensive for the publication to make any changes to such material.

Then it changed again with the introduction of phototypesetting, and if photo prints (termed "bromides") were supplied the publication was often expected to set extra lines or to replace wording, such as prices and descriptions. This changed again as the larger advertisers began, particularly with color ads, to supply film.

When copy was required to be sent electronically to publications which might be produced using a wide range of software and printed either with or without film as an intermediate medium, the major publications promoted a file format called TIFF/IT, a raster file format which overcomes the problems of line drawings and type being rasterized by having a second part of the file in vector format. It is again a system where the advertiser or the advertising agent takes responsibility, but unfortunately TIFF/IT can only be handled by top-end graphics software — it was not for the little guy.

And so came PDF...

And so came PDF or portable document format, developed by John Warnock and Charles Geschke who created PostScript through their Adobe company. This is now an almost universal format, and, initially, had the advantage for publishers of being a file format which, when used by advertisers, put the responsibility for usable copy into the advertiser's hands. These were files which were either right or not, and which could, generally, not be altered by the publisher, except that they had the advantage that their resolution suited whatever output devices they were sent to, so the same PDF could suit a high quality magazine or a coarse-screen newspaper.

Now, a number of separate applications and some plug-ins for the Adobe program which creates PDFs, Acrobat, enable an ever wider number of changes to be made to such files. The result is that while a PDF should be a final version of an advertisement, magazine publishers are being increasingly expected to make corrections and to change words and images. And so the responsibility is tending to return to the publisher.

Do what you can to resist but it is still true that advertisements provided as PDFs by those who know how to use them are easier and cheaper to deal with than advertisements sent in most other formats such as EPS (encapsulated postscript files) or as TIFF or JPEG files in which type, especially small type, is generally rasterized and therefore, at best, slightly furry or suffering from "the jaggies".

Check our web site — see page 4

As changes in this area can be fairly rapid, we will include on our web site a suggested document you may alter as you see fit to specify to advertisers how advertisements should be submitted.

Chapter 4

Producing the publication

What will you do for yourself?

With the advent of desktop publishing and its advancement to include equipment which, while much smaller than the machinery it replaces, is no longer the kind which will fit on a standard office desk, your major decision with a publication may well be to decide just how much you are going to do yourself or in your own office.

Our original "do it yourself" chapter was well back in the first edition of this book because publications were still normally produced with typewriters and drawing tools, and then passed to what in effect were large engineering works to assemble the pages and print the copies.

Ease of production has increased the number and range of publications, but it has also increased the number of poorly produced publications. If you decide to handle much of the work yourself, or in your own office, there are still skills to be learned or skilled people to be hired.

In later chapters there are descriptions of many of the processes of producing a magazine and all of the points made will apply equally if you handle any parts of the process yourself. The chapter on economics may help in deciding whether you should.

Dividing line between publisher and printer

A line that's blurred

The dividing line between publisher and printer is no longer sharp, and it is becoming increasingly common for large and small publishers to handle in their own office substantial parts of what used to be the printers' job.

Now, much of that work can be carried out with equipment you can buy from the local computer or electrical store.

But just how much should you really do for yourself? For example, page layout programs like InDesign, PageMaker and QuarkXPress will run on a more or less standard office computer, but all these programs have a fairly solid learning curve. You cannot just open the package and set to work. That is not to say that you cannot learn to use them — I have seen people who have worked wonders with a few hours of tuition, and many of the leading operators in this field were self taught.

Similarly, the almost universal image manipulation program, Photoshop, can be learned "from the book", but it takes practice, and that takes time.

Training or hiring

An option to hiring skilled people to do the work, either in your own office or at a service bureau, is to hire people who will train you while helping you create the publication. You will have to pay a higher hourly rate, but you are getting a guarantee that the work will be done and gradually preparing yourself to do it.

For the simple newsletter, however, the required skills are what is now accepted as being in the category of general office duties. Programs like Microsoft Word and Microsoft Publisher come with templates to help you prepare good quality newsletters efficiently, and there are many classes run at local community education centres which will help anyone brush up on these skills.

Even so, you may find it an advantage to hire a skilled user of such programs to prepare the templates or master files you will need, and maybe to give a general set of layout instructions.

There are also a number of low cost programs, some of them free for non-commercial use, which are well suited for quite advanced publications. You will find a list with brief descriptions and up-to-date contact details on our web site. I know of one organization which produces a very professional looking quarterly which circulates to thousands world-wide using AppleWorks (a $150 purchase).

In the layout chapter we will describe some of the points to watch, and the pitfalls to avoid — the marks of an amateur publication, such as too many different font styles and sizes, and tint backgrounds which may make the text hard to read.

Layout —
page 105
Illustrations
— page 85

In the chapter on illustrations we will describe how to ensure that you can produce photographs in photocopied publications which do not look like soot and whitewash — it is not very different from the steps which have to be taken to achieve good reproduction on the poorest quality but most widely used paper of all — newsprint.

The ubiquitous PDF

Sending to the printer

If you are producing a publication which is to be commercially printed, you will also have to decide how far you take production in your own office.

In the last couple of years there has been an almost universal change in the industry. It does not matter what software or type of computer you use to lay out the pages, the finished pages, ready for imposition will be handed to the printer as one or more PDF (portable document format) files. This now applies whether you are producing a tiny circulation newsletter for printing on a device that is really an upmarket photocopier at a shopping mall quick printer or a full color glossy magazine destined for the newsstands.

It is currently possible to produce complete artwork for the pages on a laser printer (or even an inkjet). On a very small scale you may be able to print proofs to an inkjet but improve the quality by saving files to disk to print to a top-quality laser printer at a service bureau or printer.

You may assemble pages from separate pieces of artwork. For example, have advertisements set separately and paste these on to pages which have boxes printed to indicate where the ads are to go. We will detail this process in more detail in our chapter on doing your own layout. It is seldom necessary to produce the whole of every page in the layout program.

Where the publisher is not entirely confident of the output, it is still common to output electronic files in one of several formats that can go to the printer or service bureau (see Chapter 8 on dealing with a service bureau). These application files (the actual files created by your layout program) will be opened by the service bureau or the prepress section of the printer and checked for missing items, unsuitable graphic formats and maybe to merge with files for advertisements sent direct by advertisers and agencies.

Service bureaus — page 75

In most cases the bureau or prepress department which is doing such work will then create a set of PDF files.

Imposition

Putting pages together

There are other considerations in how far you take on the production of a publication. If you are handling the layout of the pages, and production of the page layout files, do you also handle the imposition? Imposition is how the pages fit together to be printed. You can work out simple imposition for yourself — fold a sheet of paper into four and, without tearing it into separate pages, write the numbers in sequence from 1 to 8. Now open it up and you will see that pages 1,4,5 and 8 are on one side and 2,3,6 and 7 on the other. However, with more pages printed together on multi-unit presses and from several reels (or webs) of paper, the imposition can get complex and you need to ask the printer what the imposition will be.

There are other aspects you need to check too — like the gutters between pages, which on thicker publications may change slightly according to whether they are on the outside or inside of a saddle-stitched publication. The rate at which the distance between the fold and the inside margin changes from the outer pages to the inner ones is called "creep". In theory creep will change by a specific tiny amount on each spread of pages, but in practice it is common to change by specific amounts on each separate printing run which makes up the publication. The term "gutter" is also used for the space between columns.

You can check for yourself what creep is and how it is used by folding several sheets of paper in half and trimming the pages straight with a knife or a guillotine. When you open the pages flat, you will see that the top sheets are narrower than the bottom, outer, sheets.

Imposition software is expensive but there is often a compromise that the publisher will prepare "printer's spreads" of pages (putting the correct pairs together) and the service bureau or printer will assemble these into groups of 4, 8 or 16. An imposition plug-in is also available for Acrobat, working with PDFs and called Quite Imposing.

Folding, stitching (stapling)

So far this chapter has dealt with the preparation of artwork, but some other aspects of production may also be handled in-house.

If the publication is being printed on a web (or roll-fed) press, it is most likely that it will go through a folder on the end of the press, but if it is being printed on a sheet-fed press, the result will be several piles of single sheets that have to be folded, collated and stitched. Wire stitching is what office workers call stapling.

Compare the printer's cost of supplying them in this form with the full cost. You may be able to save if you collate and staple yourself, or even if you sub-contract the work. There are a lot of people keen to do a few hours casual work and speed is soon acquired. The essential tools are plenty of flat table space and a number of rubber finger stalls.

To staple, a heavy-duty stapler (Bostitch make a good range) with sufficient reach to staple along the spine, can be screwed down to a board with a fixed or adjustable back stop to allow the collated magazine to be positioned easily and quickly. With the more expensive stitchers, the folded magazine is placed over a saddle and so falls into place even more easily (hence the term "saddle stitched" which you will hear in the trade).

Newspapers do not need to be stapled, and if a magazine has only three or four sheets, you may find it does not really need stapling either.

Trimming the pages

The more pages, the more necessary it will be to trim the magazine afterwards, and this will be essential if each sheet is of eight pages or more meaning that some pages are joined at the top.

Small hand operated guillotines cost around a thousand dollars or so, though I urge caution — in the haste to get a magazine out, it is very easy to forget just how sharp a guillotine blade is. I write from experience — though fortunately I lost only the tiniest fraction off the top of a finger. New guillotines have the safety guards, but they are not foolproof.

Chapter 5

Photocopying or laser printing

Improving on a meeting notice

The next three chapters follow the progress of a magazine from the more basic methods of production to the most advanced, from photocopying to computerised processing. We start with photocopying or laser printing which might be ideal for a publication up to a few hundred copies in the home or office or up to 1000 on the kind of equipment used by a quick copy printer.

As an example, a newsletter for a small club needs perhaps a hundred copies, probably monthly. You have previously had a reminder of monthly meetings printed out from a computer via an inkjet printer and copies run off on photocopier, using standard letter, A4, legal or foolscap paper. It runs from top to bottom of each page and maybe two or three sheets are stapled together in the top left hand corner. How can it be improved?

The first possibility is to type the whole thing on half-size pages so that two pages can appear alongside each other on the full sheet folded in half and several such sheets can be stapled along the spine (saddle-stitched) to form a magazine.

You can print the master copy of each page singly and stick them together afterwards; you only have to remember whether you are typing a left or right hand page, whereas with two together you have to work out beforehand which page faces which in the finished job (though most low-cost page layout programmes will work this out for you).

Arranging the pages (imposition)

Pairing pages

This is a good point to mention how to check that the right pages are paired properly for printing. The numbers of two pages on the same side of the same sheet will always add up to one more than the total number of pages in the publication. Hence, in a 16-page magazine, pages 1 and 16 (total 17) are printed together, as are pages 2 and 15 (total 17), 3 and 14, and so on, with the centre spread being pages 8 and 9. Odd numbers are always on the right, even numbers on the left.

This works until you get so large that you have to change from saddle stitching to a square-back format, but by then you will be printing on large presses and the printer will give you what is called an imposition

Fig.5-1: What tends to happen in reproducing a photo via photo-copying is that the highlights become white and the shadows become black.

Fig.5-2: In this example, the printed output looks gray, but there are enough dots in the highlights to ensure that some will stay when copied, and there are also clear dots in the shadows, so that even with some filling in, there should not be a complete loss of detail. Because there is also a tendency for the mid-ranges to fill in, these have also been lightened. While the reproduction in the system of book printing is not one that favors quality halftones, there should be sufficient detail in this picture for you to see what the subject is.

sheet which shows exactly which pages are printed together and how they are placed in relation to each other. If you think of having page 1 on a left hand page (such as inside the front cover) I have one simple piece of advice: don't. It will drive readers crazy!

It is possible to set up the pages of a spread as columns on a page the full width of the spread — such as an A4 wide page with two columns equivalent to two A5 pages. Again, my advice is: don't. It gets too complex to keep track of where you have to type next if a feature goes from one page to another. Work to the actual page size of the magazine and use the software to put them together or do that manually.

On the office copier/printer

More about paste-up — page 141

For small circulations, you can produce quite effective publications with a computer and inkjet or laser printer and a plain-paper office copier. If you do need to print out each master copy of a page separately, or even each part of a page on its own and paste it up manually into each two-page unit, then see the chapter on paste-up for some useful hints.

You can add drawings and illustrations from newspapers and magazines can also reproduce quite well (though beware of copyright restrictions). At this stage you will have to work on a trial and error system with illustrations, learning what will work and what will not.

If you have a copier that reduces, you can prepare your original to a larger size and bring it down to foolscap or A4. This helps make the output from even the cheapest inkjet printer or low resolution laser printer look like top quality typesetting.

It also helps to use justified type, which is easier to read. Justified means that the left and right margins are even, instead of the right margin being ragged. Justification is achieved by adding extra space between words and hyphenated breaks in long words, so that the right margin becomes the same for every line (in more advanced forms of justification, spaces between letters may also be adjusted slightly).

In our illustrations chapter we deal with the problem of producing photographs which will photocopy reasonably well. Two examples of what can happen are given in figures 5-1 and 5-2 on the facing page.

About paper

It's a natural substance

You are dealing with a natural substance, paper, which is made mainly from plant fibre. It absorbs moisture from the atmosphere and reacts substantially to changes in temperature and humidity.

It will therefore behave in different ways according to the temperature and humidity. You are about to run it through a photocopier or laser printer which will heat it substantially to seal the powdered plastic and metal image to the surface. Then, often before it has time to settle back to its original condition, it will be forced through the process again to print the other side. Is it any wonder that it will sometimes crease and occasionally buckle to such an extent that it will jam? Starting from this expectation, you may be more inclined to treat the paper more kindly before using it and to be more tolerant of the occasional paper jam.

Grain in paper

Which side first?

Many paper manufacturers will indicate that one side of the paper should be printed first. This is because of the tendency of paper to curl because of its grain — and paper does have a grain just like wood, though less visible. You may find that a stack of paper which will not run easily through a photocopier will run much more easily if you turn the stack upside down. This is because paper tends to curl along the direction of the grain. On larger copiers which allow you to run smaller paper sizes in two directions — across or lengthways — you will sometimes find that paper will run in one direction and not in another.

Paper is usually cut from larger sheets such that the grain runs with the longer direction of the sheet. So the grain of an A4 sheet created by cutting a commercially available pack of A3 paper will usually run across the sheet whereas the same paper supplied as A4 sheets will run with the length of the sheet — at right angles to the sheet you cut yourself.

Conditioning paper

Let it rest

Paper should never be moved between areas where there is a substantial difference in temperature or humidity without being given several hours to rest within its wrapper to "condition" to the atmosphere in which it is expected to work. You should also try to ensure that the atmosphere where the copier is run and the paper is stored does not change dramatically, and is maintained at levels which are comfortable for the paper — which fortunately coincides with conditions comfortable for us. The makers of some recent models of copiers and printers advise against fanning the paper before putting it in the tray but it is still advisable for many. Watch a skilled printer handling paper and it is as fascinating as a baker with dough.

Although many of the more advanced copiers have duplexing units, which take a copy internally and turn it over so that the machine can print the other side, this process can lead to creasing, so you may find it better to print one side, then give the paper time to cool down and return to its normal humidity level before printing the reverse. You may also need to put a flat weight such as a large book on top to help the paper flatten out.

Chapter 6

Short run printing

Digital presses

The next step is digital printing, also known as POD (or print-on-demand) or small offset printing. These are very different processes but overlap in the fields they cover.

While most quick printing centres offer printing on digital units which are effectively large photocopiers, either black and white or color, and printing with toner, many also have small offset machines using inks. Because copiers have a relatively static cost for each copy (savings being mainly in administration time) whereas offset presses have a substantial up-front cost for making a plate but are much cheaper for each copy printed, there will be a figure for the number of copies at which the advantage moves from one to another. This will vary from one printer to another and while it is common to talk of this being at around a run of a thousand copies, this is by no means a definite figure. I have seen digital jobs come in cheaper for well over the thousand copies, and for offset jobs to win on a few hundred.

This is also an area where changes in equipment are occurring quickly.

Small offset

Convenient size

Small offset presses range from table-top machines that are little different in appearance from duplicators up to stand-alone presses which can handle, usually, up to A3 or tabloid size paper or slightly larger.

Tabloid or A3 folds in half to produce a convenient quarto-magazine format similar in size to most magazines you see on bookstalls.

The simplest system with small offset is to use a thin plastic plate which can be printed direct on many laser printers. Originally these plates required laser printers which fused the toner to the material at a higher temperature than is required for printing on paper.

Such plates cost a matter of a dollar or two, but they do have some limitations — they will not hold large areas of even tints, so you may have problems with large sizes of type and with large areas of grey even behind type. These plates are produced in a range of qualities to suit runs from a couple of hundred up to several thousand.

The next quality step is to use a metal plate for the press — it lasts much longer too. Your printer may ask you for a paper printout from your laser printer or for a kind of film — a translucent sheet like tracing paper which you print on the laser printer but with a mirror image so that the printed side can be placed against the printing plate when it is exposed to transfer the image to it. This part of the process does not have to be done in a darkroom, though it will need to avoid bright lights.

Film from an imagesetter

A further stage is to produce film from an "imagesetter" which is similar in the way it operates to a laser printer except that the image is exposed by a beam of light onto a sheet or roll of film. This film may be either negative or positive but the end result will be that it is exposed in a frame onto a metal sheet which will have a positive image and which is the plate which goes onto the press. Some larger printers have imagesetters on site, otherwise your files will be taken to a service bureau which will print them out to the specifications supplied by your printer.

Using color

You may consider using different methods for special parts of the publication. For example you may want to prepare a cover with a picture on the front and advertisements on the other pages.

On very small run publications, you may consider having an offset printed cover which stays the same for several months or a whole year.

It can be worth considering printing just the second color of a cover, such as for the title, in sufficient quantity for several issues, and then overprinting these on a black and white digital copier or photocopier.

The appearance of changed covers can also be achieved by asking the printer to use several different colors of paper "stock". He may even be able to cut his price if he can use leftovers from several bigger printing jobs. The inside pages can then be photocopied or printed on a small digital press.

The production of full color covers for short-run publications has also become dramatically cheaper in recent years using color copiers but using such methods for two colors costs exactly the same as printing in full color.

Talk to printers about whether savings can be made by grouping photographs together on certain pages, for printing on a different copier or press. The key is to use appropriate technology for the job you want to do.

I recently learned of a publisher of quite a large circulation consumer magazine who had started a separate magazine for retailers in that field. This magazine has a run of only a few hundred produced on a Docutech digital copier with the cover produced on a color copier. The individual sheets are collated in their office and stapled on a long-reach office stapler.

Digital duplicators

Stencils automated

At this stage we should also mention the digital duplicators, of which the Riso is the best known. These are related to the old style Roneo or Gestetner or even mimeo type of duplicator, where a thin wax coated paper or silk sheet was used. This stencil could be drawn on with a stylus or "cut" with a typewriter. When placed around a cylinder on the duplicator the ink is forced from inside the cylinder through the silk and through the areas where the wax has been removed onto the paper.

The digital duplicator automates this process with the stencil being created photographically as on a photocopier or direct from a computer. The stencil is also loaded onto the cylinder automatically and the old stencil removed automatically when the job is finished.

Though they usually print in just one color at a time, it is relatively simple to replace the ink cartridge with another color and run the paper through again. It can therefore produce output in two or more colors, though the registration is not accurate enough for full color work.

Lower cost

The big advantage of this method of printing is cost. While a dozen or so copies may cost more than the equivalent number of photocopies, the extra cost of further copies is minimal, often calculated in fractions of a cent per copy.

I would want to speak to users who have had the machine for longer than the standard warranty period. The small scale publisher I know who bought one to bring a twice-monthly newsletter in house was increasingly disappointed issue by issue. The firm which sold it to her had correctly said she could not do close register color but they had assured her that she could get at least "newspaper quality" halftones, and had shown her examples of that. I suspect that to achieve it she would have had to have the married the mechanic!

Once experienced, the unique smell of a duplicator printed job is unmistakable. I quite like it!

Printing tricks

Get to know the printer

There are a few other special tricks that can be effective while adding little or nothing to the cost, especially if your magazine is being printed on a small offset press.

Suggest that if the printer has been running a job for someone else in another color, that he print part of your job before washing up the press. As the wash-up is needed anyway, that should still be costed to the previous job.

Suggest too that the printer can do things such as putting different colored inks at each end of the ink duct (red at one end and blue the other produces a sort of muddy purple in the middle which gradually spreads out during a run, but for a short run you can get away with it and have three colors on the page.

On large presses, there are sometimes separate ink ducts which enable different colors to be printed at different ends of the same sheet on the one run, so this practice is quite legitimate. I have seen press operators use a piece of play dough to keep the ink colors apart for as long as possible on a small offset press.

These points bring home again the need for close contact with your printer, even if your job is small. It is most likely you will get the most co-operation from a small firm, especially one that is anxious to show what it can do.

If your job becomes one on which the printer can experiment, you may get some dramatic effects at no extra cost. An example I can quote is a small service club publication, with a run of about 100 mostly on paper plates, which came out one Christmas with greetings to members printed in gold embossed lettering.

The printer had just acquired a machine to print raised lettering in gold and other colors for wedding invitations and wanted to try it out.

We gained, and so did he because he didn't waste any money on a job that was unproductive. He also showed a hundred potential customers that he had a new service available.

Such are the things of which a small publication is made and enthusiasm is infectious. It will spread from the editor to the others in the organization and to the printer and his staff — and be reflected in a magazine which will thrill readers.

Chapter 7

On a larger scale

Sending your magazine to a printer

Now let us consider what may be called the properly printed magazine. It is now common for the printer to just have the press or presses, with the likely inclusion of a pre-press section, where completed computer files of pages will be received from the publisher, and imposed into the sets of pages in the sequences required for printing. They may offer limited services to correct problems with those files, but generally the work of assembling pages will be carried out either by the publisher or by a service bureau or graphic design house.

Service bureaus and designers may also carry through the work to the stage of producing film ready to be made into plates. However, as more printers are adopting computer-to-plate technology where the image from a computer file is sent direct to the press with no intermediate film and plate stages, it is becoming the industry norm for pages to be supplied as "portable document format" (PDF) computer files.

Using the software — Chapter 14, page 145

In later chapters we will take you through the stages of page production using your own computer equipment. This will also serve to explain what happens at a design studio or service bureau if you choose to have such specialist handle this part of the work.

Finding the right specialist

The right printer for the job

All printers specialize to some extent and so, while it is always possible that you may get good price and service in certain circumstances when you are the only magazine handled by a printer who is involved mainly in some other field, it is generally true that the best service and price will come from a printer who specializes in magazines.

Also, such a printer will probably have a few formats that best suit his equipment. He will be able to produce other formats but in general, assuming that you will be looking for the best job at the lowest price, you will be best served by seeking a format within the range the printer already knows well.

If you have an example of what you have in mind, perhaps a magazine from another publisher which is similar to the publication you are planning, give several printers a copy of it, together with a specification,

Dear Sirs

Please provide a quotation for a magazine printed on a regular basis in accordance with the following specification.

1: Frequency: Monthly

2: Run: 2000 approx

3: Publication day: 8th of month

4: No. of pages: 48 plus cover

5: Page size: 275 x 210mm

6: Paper stock: Cover to be on 100 gsm gloss coated stock, rest on 60 gsm super-calendered (alternatives will be considered, please supply samples).

7: Color: Full color required on cover only, second color on specific runs.

8: Artwork: Pages to be supplied as composite PDF files.

9: Final artwork to be in printer's hands 10 days prior to publication. Flow of pages to be as required by printer.

10: Illustrations: Grayscale pictures to be included in artwork — approx. 2 halftones per page.

11: Proofs: Blueline proofs from film are to be provided before platemaking. Press times are to be advised so that press copies can be approved.

12: Other requests: Please quote run-on per 100, and per 4 or 8pp extra. Also, cost of color inside.

13: Delivery: To be collected.

                                    Yours sincerely,

Fig.7-1: An example of how an RFQ (request for quote) might look.

but also ask for their suggestions on whether any changes will allow them to offer you a better price and or service.

Date can make a difference

A substantial cost saving can occur with some printers just by changing the date on which you want the magazine so it fits into an empty slot in their production schedule.

Most magazines come out at the end of one month showing the cover date as the next month, so most monthly magazines printers are very busy in weeks three and four of each month, but want work in weeks one and two.

Similarly weekly publications tend to come out on a Wednesday or Thursday, so if you can opt for a Monday or a Friday, many printers will give you a substantial reduction to avoid having staff and machines standing idle. Note, however, that to offer such discounts the printer needs to be sure that your job will be delivered on time.

Publications are usually printed four, eight, or sixteen pages at a time on sheet-fed presses and in much larger multiples on rotary presses, commonly 32-page sections (16 pages each side of the paper).

You need to take this into account if you expect to increase the size of your magazine. If your printer is printing eight pages at a time, it may not be economic for your magazine to grow in steps of less than that. So ask about this, or ask for the costs of running 4, 8 or 16 pages extra.

A specification

Request for quote

Figure 7-1 (facing page) shows a specification as it might be set out in an RFQ (request for quote) sent to a printer and which provides the kind of information a printer will need.

This is a relatively detailed specification, and many of the items would be decided in discussion with a printer or by giving him an example of the kind of magazine you have in mind. You must cover all these points in some way, however, to ensure you are comparing like with like. For example, you must avoid comparing a quote for a magazine where the printer will fit it in between more urgent jobs, and needs everything virtually a month in advance to one where you become the major job (if only for a few hours) and everything goes in one batch a day before you collect your final copies. So don't ask for the schedule of a daily if you can have everything ready a week early — in general the tighter the schedule, the more it will cost.

Now let us assume that you are either sending such a specification or talking over the details in order with a printer or his representative.

1: Frequency: Monthly

There is a lot of difference in urgency between a weekly, a monthly, a bi-monthly and a quarterly which, all other things being equal, can affect the price.

2: Run: 2000 approx

Fairly obvious, but if the run is likely to jump quickly to 5000, then say so and ask for a price on that too. While a run-on price is requested in this specification, no printer will want to be held to a run-on per 100 if you are likely to cut the run in half, and such a run-on price will not be accurate if the run doubles.

3: Publication day: 8th of month

As I mentioned, the publication date can affect the price, so if it is negotiable, say so — even a guide such as "first or second week of the month" will help, but be sure the printer knows that this does not mean you are unconcerned about delivery by a due date, unless that is the case.

4: No. of pages: 48 plus cover

Again, this seems obvious, but if there are likely to be substantial variations, say so, especially if it is to be seasonal, which might happen with, say, a seasonal sport, where in the off-season there may be a few token issues, that double or treble in size for the main season. Don't keep the printer in the dark, for what may seem of concern may be what appeals to him and could give you a price advantage — for example he may have other work that is at its peak when yours is down.

5: Page size: 275 × 210mm

Because printers work by standard size sheets, usually of four or eight, or even 16 times a normal magazine size page, a small change in page size may mean that the job can be printed on a different size sheet and perhaps on a different press. One printing company recently advertised the benefits of printing at their "smartsize" of 260 × 200mm instead of 275 × 210 in giving what they claim is the same reader impact at a saving, over a full year of long runs, of several tons of paper. The key was that they had access to large quantities of paper at a particular size. Common inch sizes are 11 × 8½, 10 × 8, 10 × 7½, etc.

Also the press size will have a bearing on both the size of the overall printed sheet and of the finished page. A small change in page size may, for example, allow the magazine to be printed four pages at a time instead of two, or 16 instead of eight. The running time and cost of make-ready, which is preparing the press for printing, would be the same, so the only difference in machining cost will be the cost of paper and ink, and maybe a bigger printing plate (though even the latter may be the same).

Even on web presses, some variation in page size is possible by using webs, or reels, of different widths, but the printer may only hold stocks of one standard size. He may be able to get other sizes but they would be more costly as a special order and he would always have to change reels for your job.

This is another area in which to be guided by the printer until you gain a basic knowledge of press sizes and paper sizes and can work it out for yourself.

Sometimes, of course the printer may look at the obvious course of action only. Many years ago, I managed a small offset printing business and was asked to quote on a series of jobs, some of which were too large for our press. (Yes, singular, it was that small a business).

Work and turn

I knew that a much larger business in a nearby town (which did occasional jobs for us as well) was also being asked to quote, so without giving them the full details of the job, I prepared a specification which told them how to print the job, on which press, and that it was to be printed work and turn on double-sized sheets (which means that both sides of the job are printed at once, from one plate, then the paper turned over and the other side of the sheet printed so that the opposite sides are backed up to provide two complete copies; these are then guillotined — see Figure 7-2).

The system halves the run, and as in this case the run was substantial and there was very little typesetting, it made a substantial reduction in the cost. It made so much difference that even when we added our profit margin to the job on top of theirs, we still beat their own quote They had simply run

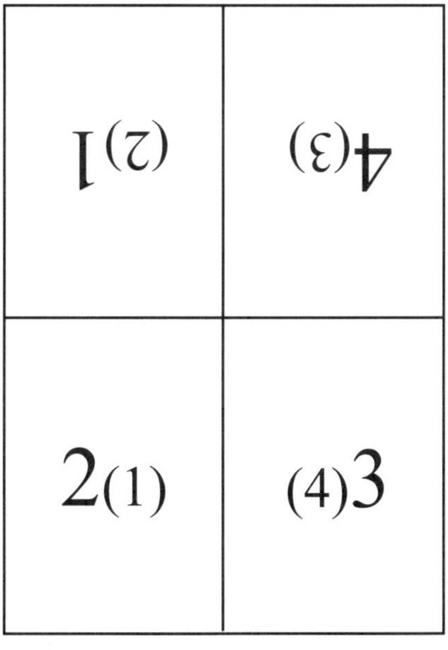

Fig.7-2: An example of how a simple work-and turn sheet might work. The large figures show how the sheet will be printed, but half way through the run the completed sheets will be turned over and run through the press again so that the same pages are printed on the back, turned so that when cut in two, each part has all four pages in the correct order. The smaller figures show the pages that are on the back of each sheet..

off their "standard" quote and had not thought about other ways of doing the job. I was not very popular with their works manager for a while, but he did eventually appreciate the humorous side of it.

There are many standard paper sizes, and different ways to fold and trim, but the finished size will depend on the trim, and that will also vary from one printer to another.

6: **Paper stock: Cover to be on 100 gsm gloss coated stock, rest on 60 gsm super-calendered (alternatives will be considered, please supply samples).**

Until you gain some knowledge of the very complicated subject of paper, it is easiest to supply samples of the paper stock you would like to have, and ask the printer whether he has something similar at a reasonable price.

Large circulation magazines use so much paper that they warrant a special order, but for smaller jobs, the printer can usually give a better price if he is printing it on a paper he usually holds in stock. This also has the advantage that he knows what it is like to use.

If the run is large, or is likely to increase, then the choice of paper can be very important from a cost viewpoint.

Paper ranges from cast-coated high gloss at the upper end through standard gloss and matt coated papers to super-calendered (which means it is smoothed by rollers only in the making, and not by adding clay or other smoothing agents) and down to the uncoated papers, of which newsprint is the best known and cheapest.

A cheap paper, however, does not always mean a cheap job — a paper that is cheap may not be identical between batches, and those small differences can cause headaches for the machinist. For example it is almost impossible to run newsprint on a flatbed press.

Weights of paper

Choosing the paper has become much easier for people in most of the world outside the USA with the introduction of standard weight measurements in grams per square metre (gsm), and with standard international paper sizes. A paper with a weight of 100 gsm is obviously heavier than a paper of 60 gsm, but things were not always so simple, and weights under the old measurements could be the reverse of what they seemed.

In most of the world outside of the USA paper is supplied in A and B sizes, with the most usual being the standard RA1 which is 610 × 860mm untrimmed and which trims to the A1 size of 594 × 841mm. This size allows for the normal folding and trimming of a magazine to A4 size (210 × 297 mm)..

There is another standard size, SRA1, which is slightly larger again to allow for publications in which the printing bleeds off the edge of the page, but where the finished job must still be the standard A4 size.

The USA and some other countries retain the Imperial measurements for paper, where weights are based on 500 sheets *in the standard size sheet in which that paper is made.*

For example, a package of American Letter size (8½ by 11 inch) office paper might be marked 20-lb. This is bond paper for which weights are based on a 17-inch by 22-inch sheet, so 500 17-inch by 22-inch sheets of this paper would weigh 20 pounds. However, with a 60 lb. cover stock that may be the weight of 500 sheets of 20-inch × 26-inch cover grade paper. To add confusion, if the weight figure is followed by a letter M, such as 120M, it will indicate that the weight is per thousand sheets rather than 500, so you divide by two.

One also had to contend with a choice between double demy and double medium that were only fractions of an inch different, and since quarto meant a quarter of a larger sheet, it could be any of at least four different sizes. I'm assured you could even order a double elephant and be met with a straight face by the paper supplier.

Heavier stock, especially card such as used for paperback books and some specialist high-quality magazines is sometimes measured by thickness in points, which is nothing to do with the printing point, being thousandths of an inch.

Check the stock

It is also worth checking whether the paper you choose is always held in stock by the paper supplier. I once made a special point of the paper being used for a new magazine, even to the extent of mentioning it in the editorial, only to be told as the job was about to be printed, that the paper was not available. Confused readers had to wait until issue number two to see the point.

If your job is being run on a web press, which means that the paper comes in rolls, then unless your run is exceptionally high, you will usually have to settle for the nearest of the standard papers the printer will use.

7: Color: Full color required on cover only, second color on specific runs.

On most presses on which small magazines will be printed, each additional color requires an additional run, but there are presses which provide color in the same run from additional printing cylinders.

If a printer has such a press he may be anxious to cover the extra costs and so will charge only a small amount extra for a second color on each sheet. This may apply to both sides of a sheet or to one side only.

More on pages that print together —
page 126

However once you put color on to one page, it costs very little extra to put color on to the others on the same side of the same sheet. So, if a 16-page magazine is being printed as two runs of eight pages on each side of a single sheet, you can have color on pages 1, 4, 5, 8, 9, 12, 13 and 16, or alternatively on pages 2, 3, 6, 7, 10, 11, 14 and 15.

If the same magazine is printed as four runs of four pages, then color on page one enables color to be printed on pages 4, 13 and 16 only. Fold some sheets of scrap paper into miniature magazines and you will see how it works.

A common way of referring to color printing is by the number of colors on each side of the sheet. Thus 4/0 will be four-color one side and blank the other (like a book cover), while 2/1 will be two colors one side and just one (probably black) on the other.

If you specify color, the printer will probably ask whether you want spot color or close register work.

Costs of close register

Close register (which means that the printing has to be very accurate) takes more time in make-ready on the press, adding to cost, whereas if small registration errors will make little difference, such as when the two colors do not touch, the preparation time is shorter. "Spot color" is usually taken to mean additional colors which do not require precise registration.

Another point on spot color — the printer will usually have a number of stock inks, and will be able to show you samples of his standard red, blue, green, etc. Depending on the amount of color printing he does, so his range will vary, but matching special colors takes time, so again, unless there is a good reason, it pays to settle for standard colors.

There are some good metallic colors now available which, although more difficult to handle than standard colors and therefore a little more expensive, do not present the major difficulties that such inks did in the past.

Full color gets cheaper

I will not go into great detail on full color at this stage except to point out that this is achieved by using three or four runs — usually yellow, magenta (a bluish red) and cyan (a light blue) with black to add depth — though occasionally the black is missed. Combinations of these four colors can represent all the colors in a normal color photograph, although for special purposes additional colors may be added. Cyan, magenta, yellow and black, commonly referred to by the initials CMYK, are the standard four color or full color system for printing. The K is variously explained to stand for the last letter of blacK or to be the "Key" color or is said to be used to differentiate it from Blue, used in the other`major color system, called RGB which is used for projection (include computer screens), where the three colors of red, green and blue together create white.

Traditional full-color is expensive because of the work needed in making color separation film from which four plates are made, and because very close register work is involved. It means that there is a high basic cost in full-color before you start running the press, so it was economic usually with large runs only.

Now there are presses which can produce short run color at more reasonable costs — usually because the image is sent direct to the printing cylinder without the intermediate stages of film and plate. These could, for example, be used for the cover of a short-run magazine.

There are many changes happening in the longer run part of the industry too such as direct imaging from computer to the printing plate with no intermediate film and much less work in preparing the job on the press.

8: Artwork: Pages to be supplied as composite PDF files.

PDF files, delivered on CD or as e-mail attachments, are now the almost universal method of sending files for printing and will become more so. However you may still use methods such as camera-ready artwork in the form of laser printed pages in printer's pairs. Spot color separations can be supplied as paper separations too, and I have seen this method used for four-color work, though only at the lower quality end of the scale, such as for printing on newsprint.

There are many ways you can supply pages for printing. They can be laser printed output either printed in pairs or pasted up. They can have illustrations in place or you can sometimes supply the pages with "keylines", outline rectangles indicating where the illustrations are to be stripped in. They can be supplied as film, produced on your own equipment or by a service bureau. They can be supplied on disk, as application files from the computer program in which you lay out the pages, or as files ready to drive an imagesetter or platemaker. However the industry is now changing and you will often hear the term PDF file ("portable document format"), also described by the name of the original program to create such files, Acrobat.

PDF files are a condensed form of PostScript, the printer control language created by the founders of the Adobe company, and have the advantages over PostScript, of being smaller, and of being independent of the output device — you can print a PDF file to anything from your home inkjet to a laser printer, an imagesetter or to a direct-to-plate or direct-to-press system, both sometimes known under the acronym CTP (for either computer-to-plate or computer-to-press).

This kind of production was described as futuristic in the first edition of this book, but it quickly became common and is now rapidly becoming the norm.

The quality from laser printers, developed from the mechanism (or engine, as it is called) of common office photocopiers, has developed dramatically. From initially being able to produce 300 dpi (dots per inch) print outs that were just about acceptable for newspaper and lower-cost newsletter use, they quickly developed to being able to produce 600 dpi, then 1200 dpi, which enables them to output illustrations with a reasonable number of greys to imitate the continuous tones of a photograph. Now there are laser printers which can output 2400 dpi — a quality of definition which had hitherto been the province of imagesetters and film.

Better quality is now expected

In our previous edition, we forecast that the increasing quality of laser printers and reducing cost would spell the end of film and plate units for all but the high quality end of the market. That hasn't happened, as we have also come to expect better quality, and film output still has a significant advantage in quality particularly for color work — and color has become much more widespread as it has become cheaper to use. The result of this has been that it has become more common to send PDF files for press output and so the laser printer, far from becoming more common in print production, is on the verge of falling into disuse!

Corrections are the problem

One problem remains — and that is a tendency for corrections, and, worse than corrections, changes to text and layouts, to extend later into the production cycle.

At one time page output would be photocopied to provide a proof for reading and correcting. It was usually read and corrected by readers employed by the printer, but it could be supplied unread, for correction by the publisher. In either case it was made clear that corrections should be kept to a minimum and that any corrections other than of errors made in the production process would be expensive.

What has now happened is that proofs are easier and cheaper and are used to make changes which should have been made at the stage of original copy being prepared. A proof should be regarded as just that — an opportunity to correct errors, not to make cosmetic changes.

9: Final artwork to be in printer's hands 10 days prior to publication. Flow of pages to be as required by printer.

Your overall cost may be partly decided by the rate at which the printer has to deal with the material. If you are supplying final pages then it will not take long for the printer to turn these into film, and even less time if they are using a CTP (computer-to-plate) system which does not require film.

Working with service bureaus — page 75

Some printers will operate normally on a much quicker schedule than others. Timing is also likely to be of greater importance when dealing with typesetting and make-up of pages, and we will deal with this in more detail in the section on service bureaus. However, don't insist on what amounts to a daily newspaper schedule if most of your copy will be sitting untouched for weeks beforehand.

On the other hand, some printers like to progress work through, one job after another, with the work to be done in one batch, at a certain time on a certain day.

In such a case your publication would be allocated a press time, usually on a fast web-offset press that may take only a few minutes to complete your run of a few thousand. If you miss the scheduled time, even by ten minutes, the next job will go on, and yours will wait until someone else misses, or until the next scheduled down-time, which could be several days later.

I have successfully put through a 4000-run newsletter for a manufacturing company on such a system. The publication looked a little silly, with one half-size paper roll running on a huge multi-unit press, and the whole job was on and off in little more than half an hour, but it did pay in costing and meant that during one exhibition the newsletter came out with a photo taken the previous day — just like a "real" newspaper.

But those are exceptions, and had that printer not known from other jobs that we could meet file delivery times, he would not have bothered quoting. We didn't ask for a quote. Based on his prices for other jobs, we told him what we were prepared to pay and he accepted the job!

10: Illustrations: Grayscale pictures to be included in artwork — approx. 2 halftones per page.

*See also
Chapter 10
— page 85*

Illustrations are the subject of a chapter on their own, so this is just a chance to mention that, under normal circumstances, you will be including all scans in the submitted artwork. If you have any special requirements, such as wanting the printer to provide a high quality color scan for the cover and to let you have a lower quality "FPO" (For Position Only) version of the file for inclusion in a disk file, then this information should be presented here.

It is also important to provide the printer with an indication of whether there will be halftone illustrations on every page, or only occasionally through the publication. This will affect his estimation of the time needed to prepare the press, as more care has to be taken to ensure good reproduction of halftones than with just text. If you are considering such usage of spot color as duotones (photos which make use of two colors to give a greater impression of depth to a picture), then you should say so, as it again has an effect on the amount of press preparation time needed in this case to ensure that the color is in exact register. Every dot of color has to be in the right place, whereas for normal spot color work, a difference of a dot or two in position is hardly likely to be noticed.

11: Proofs: Blueline proofs from film are to be provided before platemaking. Press times are to be advised so that press copies can be approved.

Proofs take time to produce (and, depending on the way the printer produces them, can be relatively costly), so don't insist on more than you really need. At this stage they should be required only to stop disasters such as a page being placed in the wrong position, or a piece of film having been lost from a spot color separation. You will usually have to guarantee approval within a very short time span so that the press is not left waiting. If you are printing on a large web press, it can be very costly to keep the press waiting — and the contracts from most printers will allow them to pass on this cost to you.

We must again stress that this is not the time for author's changes. We will have more on proofing in our next chapter, on service bureaus.

12: Other requests: Please quote run-on per 100, and per 4 or 8pp extra. Also, cost of spot color inside.

These points have been explained — but remember that if you ask for run-on costs per hundred, you cannot expect them to be accurate when the full run for the job differs by thousands from the number quoted for.

13: Delivery: To one address with manual unloading.

Remember that paper is heavy so you want your magazines delivered to where the next step will occur — wrapping, addressing and mailing them out, or to a warehyouse for newsstand distribution. If a van or truck has to be used or a transport firm hired to deliver the copies, a cost is involved. Some printers can bring in casual staff to wrap copies ready for posting at quite economic rates. Alternatively, there are mailing companies to which the copies can be delivered. Distribution is a subject in itself which will be dealt with in a later chapter.

Chapter 8

Service Bureau or DIY

Between publisher and press

Do you do the page production work yourself or use a service bureau or graphic design service? This aspect of printing and publishing is in constant flux; when I first wrote this book service bureaus did not exist, when the second edition was published there were a few printers who were beginning to separate their prepress services, by the time of the third there were thousands and now it is normal for a publisher to employ some services between their own office and the printer. Printers tend now to be the people with the presses and probably have some people who will deal with jobs which arrive as files that need some work before creating film or plate. Most page production work, if not handled by the publisher, is the work of a graphics or service bureau and some are equipped to turn out film or fully imposed files ready for plate making or for use on direct-to-press systems. Many of the service bureaus, because of the increasing call for quality means of color proofing, have entered into offering digital printing services. In this way the line between bureau and printer is again becoming blurred.

For the publisher, taking on the page production task can involve considerable outlay on computers, software and other assets, and while this may be cheaper over a lengthy period, using outside services does allow quick changes of direction for the business.

Laser output

All you need?

For some newsletters and magazines, the output from a laser printer may be all you ever need. This is sent to the printer who, for short runs, copies it on what is effectively a scanner (like that which you may have attached to your computer), or turns it into printing plates by photographing it onto film using a process camera. Other methods can include printing on to a kind of tracing paper which is used as if it was film, or direct on to the plastic plates used by small offset presses.

More on process cameras — page 86

The output from laser printers is improving to come closer to that of film output devices like imagesetters, but there may be a problem in the number of generations in the process. If the laser printer outputs to paper, that paper may have to be turned into film, which in turn has its image transferred to the printing plate. At every stage, there is some change to the shape and size of the dots which make up the image, and though it is possible to compensate for these changes to a substantial extent, it does tend to reduce quality.

This kind of problem is reduced by creating film output from laser printers directly — either using a specially developed translucent film, or with a transparent plastic which resembles normal photographic film material. In some cases these need to be passed through a chemical processor to make the black blacker but this is usually a low toxicity chemical — certainly low toxicity compared with normal photographic chemicals.

Imagesetter

Producing film

You may also purchase your own imagesetter, which include tabletop models which will fit into an office environment though you still need some training to be able to use them effectively. The film is loaded in a cartridge which is taken from the imagesetter to the processor unit where the exposed section is cut off the roll and fed through the chemicals without needing a darkroom. The cartridge with the remaining film is them returned to the imagesetter.

However, a common situation for a small publication is to provide files on disk to a service bureau which will run them through a RIP (raster image processor) to produce the film from an imagesetter.

You may also seek a graphic design service to handle some or all of the typesetting, particularly of advertisements, and perhaps the layout of pages. This option will be dealt with in a later chapter. Some or all of this work may be combined with that of a service bureau, or the whole

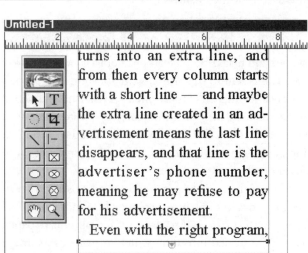

Fig.8-1: On the screen the arrow indicated in the loop at the bottom of text is red — an indication that something is missing. In some programs it is a red plus sign.

service may be provided by a printer — who may, perhaps unknown to you, send some of it out to a service bureau. However, for now we will assume that you have either produced the pages yourself or that work has been done elsewhere.

Sending program files

Many choices of software

Your pages are produced in a page layout program, which depending on your requirements and choice, is most likely at this stage to be one of the following: Adobe InDesign, QuarkXPress, Adobe PageMaker, Corel Ventura, Microsoft Publisher, or for a straightforward newsletter, maybe Microsoft Word or Corel WordPerfect, etc.

You can put these files onto a CD, one or more floppies, or a Zip disk, including any accompanying graphics files, and send them to the bureau. You can also send them by e-mail, or the bureau may have a web site set up to receive files.

This is the easiest way, but also tends to be the most expensive, and also means that you are dependent on the skills of the bureau. What they should do is open your file in the same program you used, on the same type of computer, using the same fonts, and print either directly to their imagesetter, or print to a file which contains all the print information and which then goes to a special computer folder where it waits in a queue to be printed or to be assembled into groups of pages.

That is what should happen, and what does happen in the better bureaus.

What should not happen

Unfortunately, what may happen is that your files will be opened in another program which will open the files you have created and on the bureau's normal computer platform. So your carefully crafted PageMaker files made on a PC, may be opened via a filter in QuarkXPress on a Mac, with fonts which are nominally the same as yours but perhaps made by another font maker who has very slightly different tracking or kerning widths.

The result can be that a single line in an early paragraph turns into an extra line, and from then every column starts with a short line — and maybe the extra line created in an advertisement means the last line disappears. If that line is the advertiser's phone number, he or she may refuse to pay for the advertisement.

Even with the right program, right fonts and right platform, such things can happen, though a skilled bureau operator will have a second sight for the telltale red arrows or other symbols which will tell him or her that something is wrong. With a lack of attention to detail, the errors can build to massive proportions. Ask for explanations of things which may look slightly different on a proof to what you expected; these minor differences could be acceptable, but they may indicate a workflow that could bring bigger problems.

Proofs

Ensuring things go right

You can of course insist on proofs at every stage, but it is far better to use a workflow which ensures that things do not go wrong.

One way around this is for you to produce the files ready to be printed. This involves installing the printer driver for the bureau's imagesetter on your computer and printing to a file as if you are printing to their machine. You will find descriptions of how to set up a printer in this way in the manual or help files for your computer and for the page layout program you are using.

The bureau, or your printer, will provide you with a simple text file called a PostScript Printer Description file or PPD that contains all the specifics of their printer, such as the film cassettes which are installed, the sizes which can be used, and the fonts which are already installed. You will need to refer to your manuals to see what to do with this file but it often involves just copying it to a specific folder on your hard drive, as a result of which it becomes a choice in your printer selection dialog. Many bureaus provide detailed instructions on how to do this — it is far easier than having to explain it afresh every time.

PDF files

Output from layout programs

The latest method of ensuring you provide files ready to drive an imagesetter is to create PDF files, and most page layout programs include details on how to create such files. This is a modified and compressed form of the PostScript language used in the systems described above, and produces a file which is independent of the program you used to create your magazine, the computer you used and also of the make and model of the printer you send the file to, and whether that is a laser printer, inkjet or imagesetter.

Increasingly, layout programs will create PDF files but there may be advantages in using the full version of Adobe Acrobat. One of these is that the best way to make sure you are providing the correct style of PDF is for the bureau or printer to supply you with what is called a "job options" file. This is intended for use with Adobe Acrobat Distiller. The job options file saves you entering all the detailed specifications. Let us assume that the bureau is called Apex Graphics. They will supply you with a small file called "apexgraphics.joboptions" and you will drop this in the Distiller setup folder on your computer along with the other job options files. In the

Distiller part of Acrobat you click on the arrow to the right of the "Default settings" box and select "Apexgraphics". Automatically all the settings are changed to be just what they require.

Most bureaus also have detailed forms for you to fill in to ensure you give all the information they need. This will include whether the film is to be supplied negative or positive, right reading or wrong reading, emulsion up or down (right reading emulsion up is the same as wrong reading emulsion down).

One problem which occurs with PDF files is that they are also used to produce very compact files intended for reading on a computer screen and small enough to transmit easily over the Internet. The resolution of graphics in PDF files intended for this use are much too coarse for printing, so you have to ensure that your options in creating such a file are set for the use to which the file is to be put. It is not quite a one-size-fits-all solution.

There are still bureaus and printers who are wary of accepting PDF files, and will tell all kinds of horror stories of their early use. That this is no longer true may be seen in the increasing number of printing and publishing companies which will accept only PDF files, or which now charge more for jobs provided in any other form.

Tint percentages

Getting what you expect

A good bureau will regularly calibrate their equipment to ensure that a 10 per cent tint output from a PostScript file will be a 10 per cent tint (give or take perhaps one per cent) on the film they produce. However, *you* should also ensure that what you expect from a specific tint is what they will output — *your* equipment may not be calibrated, or not calibrated in the same way. So it is a help to give a bureau some examples of the tints you expect and see whether you agree. It may be easier for you to change.

When you are providing PostScript or PDF files to a bureau it is reasonable to assume that the same file to your PostScript laser printer will produce the same results. There are some technical reasons why it might not, but they aren't common and the bureau should be able to tell you what is happening or not happening. It is usually involved with the massive extra processing power needed to process complex drawings — and that curves are in fact made up of large numbers of straight lines, referred to by a "flatness" setting.

Remember too that a large illustration dragged in a layout program to occupy just a small space still has the same amount of information; it will often be worthwhile to reopen such graphics in a program such as Photoshop and reduce the image to more closely match the size finally used. A good bureau will advise you on how to do this work for yourself.

Working in color

**Proofs
are the
key**

When you move to working in color, there is not only a need to see what will separate on to each color plate — something you can see by printing each color separately to a black laser print — but also a need to be able to see what the final color job will look like. This involves color proofing and this is an area where more developments are still needed, and where at present you have to balance the assurances you want against the price you are willing to pay.

We have referred to blueline proofs, which is the common name still for the proofs which look like the copies of architects' plans, and which, as with those plans, are now usually grey and yellow rather than blue and white. These are now also known as dylux proofs and though they are cheap and much easier to read than negatives, they are contact proofs made from the film, and therefore the film has to be made first, and remade if a mistake is discovered. They are good for spotting any errors in halftone screening but not for color.

Among the cheapest proofs are digital color proofs, printed to either a large format inkjet printer or in sections or tiles to a color laser printer. They are produced either from the application files or from the PostScript or PDF files to be sent to the imagesetter and so can fail to show up any problems that will only show in the imagesetter output. Colors were never very accurate but there is new software which improves this dramatically. Another problem with digital proofing is that many systems will cope happily from the application files when a color image is in RGB rather than CMYK format, but an imagesetter will usually output only a grayscale image from an RGB image.

**Seeing
proofs on
screen**

Even cheaper, if the bureau will let you do it, is to see the images on the screen of the imagesetting equipment. All recent raster image processors (RIPs) let the job be seen on screen, usually in color and as separations, before it is actually run to film and some page layout software is now offering similar on-screen previews. This lets you easily see if there are incorrect numbers of colors (such as a spot color left in a job which should be all process colors), missing registration marks or wrong rotation. The imagesetter operator should be skilled enough to compare what he sees with what you have provided (maybe an inkjet color print) and should enable you to spot errors such as the RGB image mentioned above.

Other proofs are known by trade names such as Cromacheck and Cromalin, the latter being the original chemical proof. Both systems allow for progressive proofs, which is important if you are printing on single or two color presses as you can combine overlays to see how the output should look after each of the colors is printed.

Chapter 9

Producing the pages

Changes happening now

Production of large scale magazines is changing dramatically, with many introducing systems based on equipment little different to that which you can have in your own office or home.

The difference is in the size of networks for computers and in overall file management through what are called integrated systems.

These enable copy to be entered by the journalist, viewed by department and senior editors, transferred to queues (actually special computer directories or folders) according to the section of the publication in which they are to appear, and then to particular page queues. They will be edited by sub-editors who add codings for all typesetting changes, and then referred back to a senior sub-editor who will check details and transmit the copy to a design and layout section

Similarly the ads will be prepared in a variety of programs and saved in formats which can be brought into the page layout system.

This can require dozens of terminals and several server computers with massive storage capabilities that, with daily newspapers, will store the total input of agency news services for several days, together with the current, last edited and original versions of every story. All advertisements likely to be repeated or used as a basis for new ones will also be stored.

As you have at home

However, the basic equipment used and the computer programs used on a much smaller publication, even one run from a home office, may well be identical. The computerisation of accounts and mailing lists will be dealt with in the later business chapters of this book.

It may be worth noting that even when I was writing the first edition of this book in 1984, I was able to send text files of extracts from the book for comment to some people by sending it via an acoustic modem that clipped to a standard telephone handpiece and that I stored a backup copy of the text on a mainframe computer via a communication service that was a forerunner of the Internet. I used packet switching to reduce the cost of a call from a tiny rural community in Western Australia to little more than a local call. This was 20 years ago.

Now I hardly wonder at being able to send sections of this book to experts across the world for their comments at negligible cost.

I am able in a home office to have some of the most powerful page layout software that does more than was possible in the equivalent of a substantial engineering works when the first edition of this book was written.

Still advancements continue — the latest being in the handling of graphics, so that most output for publication is in digital form all the way from the camera to the press. The ease of working with color has also improved dramatically. We have perhaps reached a point where prices may not reduce further, but the quality and abilities of what we will expect for those prices may yet soar.

Organising information

Keeping files so they can be found

I have found, however, that while computers used in any aspect of publishing enable a lot of information to be stored, and access to that information obtained fairly quickly, too often very little thought is given to the arrangement of that information.

For example, computers with large hard disks can become unwieldy unless at least a little thought has been given in advance to the structure of directories and the ways in which files are named.

While it is now possible to use the whole of a large disk drive as a single logical disk drive, it will often make life easier if it is divided into at least two logical drives: for example drives C: and D:, with C: being used for programs and D: for data files such as editorial and advertisement copy, or even for letters and invoices.

The difference between a physical and logical drive is that while the actual computer mechanism may have only one disk drive unit, usually called drive C: on a PC (or anything you like on a Mac), this may be divided so that, as far as computer programs are concerned it appears that you have several drives, each a fraction of the total physical drive size. Then when you need to back-up those files, just in case something goes wrong, you only have to back-up drive D:, because your original program disks have already been backed-up and remain unchanged.

Naming helps deletion too

Similarly, a little thought to the naming of files will enable you to easily spot which files are advertisements, and have to be kept for future use, and which are editorial and can be discarded.

A suggested system in which all editorial publication files begin with the letters ED would make it simple to automate their deletion after the end of a month by using a batch file, or by highlighting all such files in a file manager program and shifting them to a Trash subdirectory ready for deletion the following month or for storage on a separate backup disk.

Consideration should be given to the way your programs move between directories when offering selections from which to open files, place text and artwork files and so on. Some programs will offer the choice from the last directory selected, others will always return to a default directory. Much time can be wasted changing to other branches of a complicated directory structure. And this applies whether you are using computers just for word processing and accounting or whether you are using them for all stages up to the production of print-ready files.

Advertisement files

Keep track with key numbers

There should also be some planning of how you are going to store advertisement files. This can be as simple as giving each advertisement a number in a database program you use to keep track of the bookings. That number can form part of the name of the file in which the advertisement is prepared. Other information in the filename could indicate the original date, the person who typeset the ad, the publication name or any other details which will enable you to find the artwork. The message is: keep it simple — just enough complexity to do the job.

All or part of this information can be included in a file reference or key number printed in the smallest possible type within the advertisement. You will see such key numbers in the advertisements of many publications.

At the most sophisticated level of production, there are advertisement booking systems which will allocate such reference numbers, print out booking sheets for specific issues (which will list all the ads booked for that issue with any special requirements on positions), and even prepare dummies showing where each advertisement will go, based on the instructions entered into the system.

Some such systems can also prepare the page layout files with frames already drawn in to indicate the advertisements, and may even include the ability to call in the advertisement copy automatically based on the text details entered in the ad frames — this can be done at an early stage or after the editorial copy has been placed in position.

More on automation — page 150

Simpler automation systems are also available which enable the person who is operating the page layout software to draw in frames to indicate where the ads will go and the name of the file containing that advertisement. A script or simple program can then call in and place the copy for that advertisement, for all the advertisements on a page, or for all those in that issue. Some of these systems work with several different layout programs, while others have to be specifically written for a particular program.

For the small operator the message is simple: do it manually but ensure the information you use will let you locate the files when you need to find them at a later time.

Back up your files

When a computer crashes

Another aspect to consider is back-up of your files to ensure you still have the information when a computer crashes. The issue you are working on should be backed up at least daily in some way to media which can be held away from the computer. For someone preparing only the editorial, this may be onto a few floppy disks. Otherwise it may need a Zip disk, or a tape backup system or a means of writing to a CD or DVD. You could also consider a second, removable hard disk and a file writing system which duplicates on that everything written to the main hard drive.

You should also consider keeping a copy off the premises so that in the event of a fire you will never lose more than a day or two's work.

Similarly you may keep a second copy of backups of previous issues at another site if you are likely to need such material for future issues.

Insurance may play a part in ensuring the future of a business but no insurance payout will help you to get back in business the next day, whereas a borrowed computer and a set of backup disks will keep you going.

Chapter 10

Illustrations

A major part of most magazines

Pictures and line drawings form a major part of most magazines, unless you are restricted to the most basic of typewritten newsletters.

With a photocopied or small-offset magazine or newsletter, you can paste up line drawings that are the same size as the finished job — or which will be reduced by the same proportion as the rest of the material. Provided the original has good contrast, which is to say a sharp definition between black and white or red and white, it should reproduce well.

Red reproduces as black by most photographic processes, and light blue does not reproduce at all. This means that guide lines and marks can be printed, written or drawn in light blue, and you can color red anything you want to reproduce black, which comes in very useful if *you* need to see the information beneath to ensure it is exactly where it should be. Art supply shops still sell sheets of "Rubylith" or similar plastic material on which the thin red coating can be cut or scraped away to reveal the transparent base material.

Pencil drawings do not reproduce very well at all, unless you regard them in the same way as photographs, which will be dealt with later in this chapter.

You may be able to reproduce photos from newspapers as these are made up of quite coarse dots, but the finer screen of magazine photographs may present problems.

Sometimes there is enough contrast in a proper photograph to reproduce well even when the gray areas either drop out to white, or fill in to black. This is an effect used often in magazines, but has to be accepted on a trial-and-error basis — try the picture in an ordinary photocopier; if it looks reasonable, you will probably get a similar effect in printing.

Plates can make a difference

Some of the systems used by small offset printers work well in reproducing the fine detail of photographs and detailed line drawings. But some printers, in order to keep their costs to a minimum, use plates and platemaking equipment that cannot produce fine detail. Usually, if this is true, they also have problems in reproducing large solid areas, as with the larger sizes of heading types.

In many cases, the printer, if he does not have the equipment to make the better quality (and slightly more expensive plates) usually has an arrangement with another printer to make them for him. However, be wary of major increases in costs — faced with charges of more than a couple of dollars for each of several illustrations, you should be getting other quotations.

See page 63

You can reproduce photographs in full detail by the small offset process, but in effect, you are then using the same facilities as with the printing described in "On A Larger Scale" in chapter six. Therefore we can move on to a general description of how a photograph gets into print.

While photographic paper reproduces all shades of grey that come between black and white, any part of an image that is printed has to be at one extreme or the other, either solid black, or an unprinted area. Therefore we have to achieve the impression of shades of gray by other means.

Screens and dots

Round dots from square holes

Fortunately, it is a simple, yet unexplained, principle of physics, that if you put a close-mesh grid of fine straight lines, drawn at right angles, on a transparent sheet of material, over a negative when you re-photograph a picture, your resultant image is made up of round dots, varying in size according to the darkness of the original areas between the lines.

Although it is becoming less common, many printers will still have a darkroom, like a photographer's darkroom, but with a very large piece of equipment called a process camera. It may appear extremely complex, and some have groups of dials and digital read-outs that seem at first glance to be beyond comprehension.

Take another look, for it is really just a very large version of the old bellows-style Brownie that set Eastman-Kodak on their road to fortune. The image to be converted to a screened illustration is on a surface near the floor, usually covered with a sheet of glass to keep it flat, and it is illuminated by several floodlights. Above this is a lens on a large bellows, that is raised and lowered by hand or motor. Above this again is a place to put the material you are creating, which is kept in close contact with the "screen" and another sheet of glass by an airtight cover attached to a small vacuum pump. The screen may be glass or plastic and is a transparent sheet with a grid of fine lines drawn or etched on it. Most printers would have several screens, of different degrees of fineness to suit different qualities of work and qualities of paper for the finished job.

The output of such process cameras can be film or a screened paper print known as a bromide or screened bromide or by the Kodak brand-name of PMT. Because this bromide has to be photographed again to make a printing plate, it is usually developed to give a rather washed-out image and the full contrast returns only with the finished job. To achieve this washed-out look, part of the exposure will have been in the form of a "flash" which ensures that there are separate dots even in the most solid areas.

The finished halftone, so called to distinguish it from the full-tone of a normal photograph goes to the make-up bench in the comp room to be pasted up along with the typesetting.

At the other end of the scale, it is possible to project a normal photographic negative in an enlarger onto halftone negative paper with a screen over it. By this method there is no intermediate continuous-tone print.

Line illustrations

The scanner moves in

The process to make a line illustration was similar to that used for a halftone except that no screen was needed. If you have a line illustration (such as a cartoon or drawing which uses no gray tones), and you want to use it the same size, the original can be pasted straight down onto the layout.

You may also be able to use a reducing photocopier to produce a line drawing of the right size at a fraction of the cost of a bromide.

That's all the "old" way of doing things — not used as often as it once was, but not yet completely replaced.

It is now more usual to use completely electronic systems in which an original is scanned on what is logically called a scanner. This is rather like the top deck of a photocopier but the information about the image, instead of being transferred to paper is sent as a digital signal to a computer and can be stored as a disk file.

However, many of the skills in producing a good scan are the same as those which were needed to produce a good bromide — a point which is often forgotten. There still has to be regard to the range of tonal differences in the original, and the purpose for which the photo will be used.

The output files from scanners can be resized and adjusted in many other ways using a wide range of illustration software on any computer with a high resolution graphics display.

Digital cameras

Photos as files

The latest development is in digital cameras which produce a computer file instead of an exposed roll of film. Each picture is a separate file which can be read into a computer illustration program and adjusted in the ways described above.

Beware of photo prints made on inkjet printers. They can look to be of similar quality to a normal photographic print, especially those produced by some so-called "photographic-quality" inkjet printers. However, the image is already made of dots and they will clash with the dots created when such pictures are scanned and printed again.

To overcome this, you can try the following method: scan the print at the highest resolution your scanner will allow, and, in your image editing software, apply a fairly massive amount of blur. This will tend to merge the existing dots. Now you can reduce the size of the image and try reapplying a minimal amount of sharpening. You may also like to try scanning the print at a slight angle to ensure that the angle of the dots in the print will not clash with the dots in your final output.

However, it will be much easier and often quicker, to ask the person supplying the print for a copy of the original computer file from which it was printed.

Pictures in word processor documents

Getting them out

Another problem you are likely to encounter is the submitted article in word processor format which includes the illustrations. Sometimes it is as easy as copying the illustration, opening a new file of suitable size in a program such as Photoshop and pasting it in. On other occasions, I have resorted to printing the file to PostScript, creating a PDF (portable document format) file and then importing this into Photoshop to crop to size.

Scanning resolution

Having mentioned resolution, we should mention the part played by resolution in general. Scanner manufacturers will often quote a massive figure for resolution, but you need to ask what is the "optical resolution" of a scanner as increased figures can be produced by interpolating dots between those the scanner actually produces. While this can be done within the scanner, it is usually best done, if needed, within the more advanced image software such as Photoshop.

And while you need a high resolution to scan line artwork, for halftone scanning you will seldom need the highest resolution offered by even the cheapest of scanners. More important is the bit depth (the number of bits used to store picture information) and even more important, the dynamic range. The latter can be compared to the quality of a lens in a camera.

Scan at twice the dpi

So, what resolution do you scan at? The most common working rule is to scan at twice the resolution you will print at. For instance, if you will be printing using a screen of 133 lpi (lines per inch), a fairly good quality (newspapers use 85-105 lpi, for example) you will not need to scan at more than 266 lines per inch. This is based on the original and final sizes being the same. You may find that scanning at 1.5 times, or even 1.2 times the final resolution is all you need. You can always adjust the size in your graphics program.

As mentioned, some allowance has to be made for the comparison between the size of your original print and the size it will be used. If you are reducing the picture to half size, you can scan at half the resolution. You may need to compromise if you are not sure whether there may be a slight change to the eventual size. In such case it is better to err a little on the side of conservatism, and perhaps have a file which may be just a little larger than needed.

If a picture intended to be used for a full page is to be used only for a thumbnail, then it will pay in processing time, for proofing and for eventual output, to open the photo in your image editing software and reduce the image size.

Sharpening pictures

'Unsharp' masking

Another aspect of scanning is sharpening. I will not go into details here of why the most effective method of sharpening is actually called "unsharp masking" except to say that it achieves electronically an effect which was used for decades by photographers.

However, there is a some misunderstanding of the three settings used in sharpening.

Sharpening works by increasing the difference between light and dark at any edge in the image where there are such differences. The pixels at the edge of an object may become darker and those pixels immediately adjacent to the pixels which become darker become lighter.

The three settings which control sharpening are amount, radius and threshold. Amount is fairly obvious — the more you sharpen, the greater the edge effect you get. However, this tends to produce a halo around objects. Radius restricts this halo effect to a specific number of pixels, so a smaller radius will reduce the halo effect. Threshold specifies how far apart tonal values have to be before the sharpening will be applied. A higher threshold setting will apply sharpening to less of the picture, and will ensure that smooth gradations are not affected.

For fairly low resolution work on cheaper quality papers, we usually start with fairly high amounts, 250 or more in Photoshop, radius of 1 or less, and threshold of around 4. Higher quality work will usually require less sharpening.

There is another application of the word threshold in working with illustrations. This is when converting grayscale to bitmap and is the level at which gray converts either to black or to white.

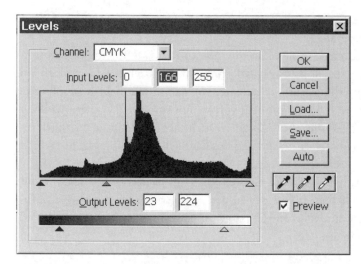

Fig.10-1: There may need to be fairly dramatic moves between input and output levels for an illustration to cater for dot gain, and the tendency of highlights to drop out and for dots in shadows to fill in. Changes are less necessary as quality of printing and paper improves, but they are always necessary to some extent.

Allowing for dot gain and dropout

Ink spreads

An aspect of image work which has to be made more definitely for printing on cheaper papers at lower resolutions is the amount by which allowances have to be made for the changes to dot sizes which occur in the printing process.

Let us take the cheapest of papers as an example: newsprint. This requires substantial changes very similar to those required in reproduction by photocopying.

In such situations, the dots in highlights tend to drop out to print just white, while at the other end of the scale, the dots in shadow areas tend to fill in to become solid black. The answer is to ensure that the smallest dot in the original is large enough so that when printed, while it becomes smaller, it still leaves the hint of a dot. At the other end of the scale, shadows will have dots which have sufficient white areas between them that even when they fill in, they will leave just a hint of white. (In actual fact, dots usually change their shape around the mid point of the scale, so that dots in white areas are small black dots, and dots in dark areas, instead of being huge black dots, are in fact small white dots.)

There is another problem with such printing and that is what is called dot gain. Through the process and particularly in the final stage where ink adheres to the image on the printing plate, and is then offset onto a blanket roller and then onto the paper, it tends to spread. It spreads furthest on lower quality paper.

Gamma settings

The way around this is to allow for the dot gain by what is called a "gamma" setting in your image manipulation program. Your printer should be able to tell you the figures for gamma settings and also the minimum and maximum dot sizes that your illustrations should contain. If your printer cannot give you this information, there are some inbuilt settings available in programs such as Photoshop according to the type of paper you are printing on.

Figure 10-1 shows a dialog box from Photoshop in which some fairly drastic changes have been made for an image being prepared for printing on relatively poor quality paper. You will see that both sliders at the bottom of the output scale have been moved in and that the central slider in the input levels has been moved to the left to change the gamma setting. The changes have to be made too for better quality papers, but they are much less drastic.

Line artwork

How high do you go?

I mentioned that line artwork should be scanned at as high a resolution as possible, up to the resolution of the final output device. However, you may find that you can see little difference between line art scanned at 1200 dpi, and the same scanned at 2400 dpi. If so, then opt for the lower resolution.

Remember too that line illustrations are often printed at a much smaller size than the original, and so can be scanned at a proportionally smaller resolution. You might scan a logo which is to be used at 25 per cent of the original size at 300 dpi because when reduced in the page layout software it will actually be giving you 1200 dpi.

This brings you close to the definition of an office fax machine, so you can sometimes have a logo increased in size on a photocopier, faxed to you at the fine setting, and then reduced while scanning, to give you reasonable reproduction — and much cheaper than a courier.

Getting the pictures you want

That explains how the illustrations are made, but a far more important aspect is how to specify what you want. Even professional photographers are not always aware of what is needed in a print for reproduction. I have seen photographers who make a good living at wedding photography produce a poor quality print for a newspaper and then claim that bad reproduction is the newspaper's fault.

Avoid 'soot and whitewash'

Firstly, a print should be glossy, not matt, with good contrast, but not so much so that it becomes what is known as "soot and whitewash", losing all the tones between the highlights and the darkest shadows. It need not be a large print, but should not require excessive enlargement.

It should also be remembered that it is unusual to use the whole of the print area of a photograph when it is reproduced. Try covering both sides and the top and bottom of any photograph you have handy, and see just how much can be covered before you start to lose a full impression of what it is a photo of. Even photos of groups of people can usually be trimmed on each side by a little, and the top and bottom can usually be brought in substantially.

Few amateur photographers get close enough when taking pictures of people, so it is not uncommon to find that even though the original picture of a presentation, may be about 150mm (6″) wide, the image area that you will want to use may be half that or less — and need blowing up considerably.

Later in this chapter we will look at how to calculate the depth of a picture for any given width (or the other way round), but in specifying pictures, ask the photographer to look for either a vertical or horizontal picture when he or she is taking it. These look considerably better than a square picture, but remember that the actual print proportion does not matter — it is the part of it which you are going to use which is important.

Cropping photos for different spaces

Many ways to trim

A good photographer who is used to producing pictures for magazine reproduction will ensure that the image is large within his print, but at the same time he will allow a little space for trimming, as the proportions of the image as he sees it may not exactly suit the magazine layout.

As an example that comes from being responsible for six publications at the same time, overlapping in some of their coverage, I have used the same photograph and story in many different ways.

Fig.10-2: The same picture, but filling very different spaces.

Fig.10-3: Two L-shaped pieces of paper can help you to visualize what a picture will look like when cropped.

For example, a single shot of a woman sitting in an armchair has been used for a head shot (requiring some enlargement), a wide picture of the woman down to arm level, and as a full length vertical illustration — all from the same print. Similarly, a scenic picture of a road disappearing into distant hills has been used as a very shallow distant picture, and as a very narrow but tall picture of the road, cut in hard on the sides.

Our example here (Figure 10-2) shows a koala depicted in three ways — firstly the full shot, then two close crops.

There is considerable skill in being able to look at a picture and see the many ways in which it can be used. It is however a skill that comes from experience, and a few sheets of white paper to enable you to cover parts of the picture are the best guide. You can also cut out two big 'L' shapes cut from ordinary sheets of copy paper as shown in Fig.10-3. Do not forget that a picture can also be trimmed in unconventional ways — maybe at an angle, or with a rectangle taken from it at an angle.

Cut-outs and deep etches

Partial cut-outs can be effective

You can also use a cut-out or partial cut-out of a picture, still often known by the letterpress term of deep-etch. A quick glance at any newspaper will show many cut-out pictures in advertisements, ranging from heads to cars. The latest versions of image handling software such as Adobe Photoshop have made it much easier to produce the "masks" needed for such cut-out illustrations.

However, there are still publications where it is common for a part of the bromide or even a picture output on a laser printer to be cut out of the screened image by a compositor using a scalpel.

Sometimes, rather than cut out the entire image, it can be effective to have just the top of a head or something else that comes to the edge of the print cut out so that it extends beyond the rectangle of the picture on the page.

If the edge is difficult to see on the original photograph and you are going to create a cut-out picture it can be useful to prepare a simple paper mask to place over the picture before it is scanned.

Look at the background

A major point in taking pictures is to remember the background. There is a tendency for the amateur taking a picture of, say, a presentation from one person to another, to ask the two people to stand against a wall or close by some object. You will have seen pictures of people who seem to have plants growing from their head, and ugly brick walls that dominate a photograph.

If instead of looking for such a background you move the people forward, so that the background becomes just that — and far back — it will be out of focus, and therefore the people will become more dominant. You will need to refer to photographic books to learn how to use depth of field, but this is a very important part of the art of photography in terms of ultimate publication.

Award-winning photographers may also produce excellent prints of subdued tones, but these need to be reproduced by equally good means of printing, using high quality art paper and top press work and platemaking.

Such subtle work is possible, but usually there is a considerable loss in contrast with the change from full tone to halftone, making the tones difficult to control. This should be remembered when considering any print for publication. Again, if you have an enthusiastic team you can get some remarkable results from indifferent prints. I have seen results that are better than the original — but not very often. On the whole, if the original looks good, the result should be reasonable.

Reproduction from printed material

You can reproduce pictures from printed material in two ways.

You can treat the printed picture as if it was an ordinary original, although remembering that you cannot blow it up very much, or the original screen will become visible. Scan the print at a high resolution and use the filters of your image editing software to blur the image so that the individual dots disappear before you then reduce the resolution and resharpen the image. This will help reduce the patterns which result when a new screen is applied to an image which already has such a screen. This is called a moiré pattern and can also be reduced by scanning the picture at an angle. You may need to experiment to see what angle is most effective.

You can see moiré patterns if you place two very fine pieces of material one over the other and look through them. As you change the angle between one weave and the other, you will see patterns appear and disappear. These can become very obvious and distracting if they occur in rescreening a photo. They can also happen if there are strong patterns in the photo, such as may occur with tartan materials and lace curtains.

If the screen of the original (the number of dots in any given area) is similar to that used in your magazine, you may be able to reproduce a black-and-white illustration by reproducing the dots from the original. This dot-for-dot, as it is called, tends to fill in on the dark areas, and to drop out to white on the light areas, but it is sometimes possible, and does overcome the moiré problem mentioned above. You could even make a feature of the dot pattern to stress that it is a picture reproduced from, for example, a historic document.

There is however, another warning in trying to reproduce from existing printed materials — beware of infringing copyright, a problem that will be referred to in a later chapter on legal problems in general.

Clip art

Quality is mixed

Clip-art is another useful source of illustrations. Clip-art comprises collections of drawings and parts of drawings which you can mix and match to produce a wide variety. They used to be printed on sheets ready to be cut and pasted onto artwork (hence the term "clip"-art) but are now available as images on computer disks.

There are very mixed standards but some of the collections extend into a million or more items, at which level you need to ensure that the images come with an easy means of searching for whatever you may need.

As has already been mentioned a large amount of "clip art" is available on disk, and the clip art libraries that used to issue regular packages of illustrations on a variety of subjects now put out the same kind of illustrations on disk. These include photographic illustrations as well as line drawings and the photographic images often come complete with ready made clipping paths so that they can be laid over any kind of background.

There are also programs that will easily fit type to curves, slant type, add shadows, etc.

If you are using many pictures, keep a file of head shots, which are always useful to fill an empty space as well as brightening otherwise dull pages and being necessary to show who you are writing about.

For filing prints of such pictures, a simple card index with the pictures attached to the cards with a spot of rubber solution is the system I have found most effective, but you may well decide on a different one. If you do not want to cut heads from bigger pictures, then you may like to keep group shots in numbered order and make a note of the print number in the index file.

A filing drawer of manila folders marked with general subjects is useful for other pictures. And don't do as was done by the filing clerk on one newspaper I know, and throw out pictures when someone dies — you may well need them later on.

You may also like to keep a file of useful line illustrations —especially ones connected with your special field. For example, if it is a magazine covering a particular sport, keep line drawings you come across of that sport, the equipment and so on. If it is a club with a symbol, you will want that in different sizes, and so examples cut from any printed letterheads and leaflets will come in useful, unless you have a full range of digital images.

You can set up electronic storage which mimics this physical storage. Add a caption including the date the picture was taken and where, description of picture, including names and, if necessary, relationships, and dates the picture was used. Include a category and indication of date taken and contents of the picture in the file name. As the numbers of pictures increase you may consider using one of the programs designed for keeping track of pictures and artwork or use a database file you create for yourself.

Because of the tight schedule required in print production, there is not time to sort out many small problems as they arise. Avoiding them by having everything ready in advance, and not relying on things being where they should be will avoid many of those last minute panics — there will be enough of them caused by things that cannot be foreseen.

Sizing pictures

They change in both directions

I have mentioned the useful method of checking how much of a picture is needed by placing sheets on white paper over the print in many different ways, but what seems to be the biggest problem with illustrations is calculating what size and proportion they will be in the finished publication.

The major point to remember is that if a picture is reduced or enlarged in one direction, then a proportionate change will take place in the other dimension. To put it at its simplest, if the height of a picture is halved, then the width will also be halved. Any other choice of dimensions will change the content of the picture.

It is now most common to accurately size a picture after scanning, by reducing one dimension to that which is needed and then reading the computer calculation of the other dimension. However, there is still often the need to calculate the printed dimensions of a picture before it is scanned.

The simplest way of finding the final size is by using a diagonal line, as shown in Figure 10-4. Press the point of a pencil into the top margin of the print at the extreme left and right sides of the area you want to use. Similarly, press the point into one of the side margins to show the top and bottom of the area you want to use.

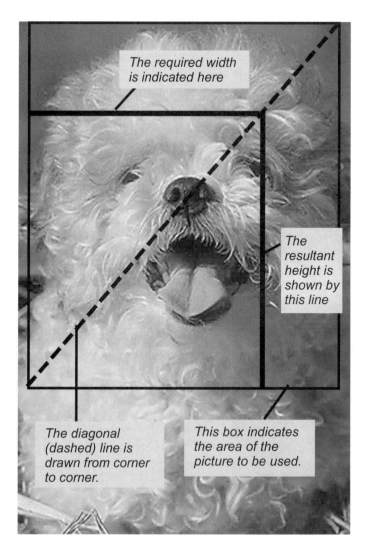

The required width is indicated here

The resultant height is shown by this line

The diagonal (dashed) line is drawn from corner to corner.

This box indicates the area of the picture to be used.

Fig.10-4: Lines drawn on the back of the picture to indicate the part of the picture which will be used — in this case a close crop on the dog's head. Then draw a diagonal line across this area. Now find the place along this diagonal where a horizontal line is the required width (slide a rule up and down to find where that place is) — and from that point to the bottom shows the resultant height of the picture. The larger box shows what the content of the picture will be; the smaller box shows how big the picture will be when reduced in proportion.

Turn the print over and, on the back, draw, very lightly in pencil, lines down and across from the pimples which will have resulted from the pencil pressure. You now have a rectangle containing the area of the print you want to use. Draw a diagonal from the bottom left to the top right. Now measure across from the left hand vertical line and slide your rule up or down until the distance from that line to the diagonal is the width required in the finished job. Put a small tick across the diagonal line at that point. Measure down from the tick to the bottom horizontal line and that will be your finished height.

You can use a light table as a refinement to see the picture through the back, or there may be a handy window which you can put the picture against to serve the same purpose — or even just hold it up to the nearest light to see where to put your marks on the back.

You should use a pencil on the B side of HB to avoid marks which can be seen from the image side of the picture and you may need to draw the lines more than once to decide on just which parts of the picture you want to use in order to end with a particular final size.

You can use two rules placed on the front of the picture to serve the same purpose, using one as the diagonal and the other to measure the horizontal and vertical dimensions.

This is a good initial step if there are a number of options, and was

Fig.10-5: Old fashioned tools. Two proportion calculators, commonly known as "wheels", and a pair of proportional dividers. The lower wheel, a cardboard one, has a cutout window showing the percentage, while the upper one, in plastic, has separate indicators for setting depth and width — once these two are set, they can be moved together over the back wheel to show the depth for any required width.

probably the most common method on many publications before the cuts on the picture were drawn on the front with a red or black chinagraph pencil — or with a white chinagraph on a dark picture. Chinagraph was used because this waxy crayon-like material could be easily removed with cotton wool or just with a piece of copy paper screwed up.

However, some process departments did not like chinagraph marks because they came off on the glass of the process camera and they preferred all marks to be either on the back of the photo or in the margin. For similar reasons, marks on the front of a photo should not be in a form which can come off on the glass of a scanner. One common way now is to use removable Post-It type notes to indicate where pictures are to be cropped.

Proportioning wheels
The method of calculating proportions that I prefer is by the proportioning wheel, available from any print supply house. This consists of two concentric discs of either card or plastic.

The original size on one scale is placed against the required size on the other, and, whether this is the height or width, then the other dimension can be read off by seeing what lines up against the original measurement of the other dimension.

For example, on the cardboard one I have in front of me at the moment the original size is set on the inner scale against the desired size on the outer scale. If I have an original picture that is 54 ems wide and want a screened print 20 ems wide, I set 54 on the inner scale against 20 on the outer scale. The original picture is 20 centimetres deep, so I look at 20 on the inner scale and against this is 7.5 on the outer scale, so the original of 54 ems by 20 cm will become 20 ems by 7.5 cm. You can also use the scales to indicate inches.

Mixing measures
This also shows how different units of measurement can be mixed. But — and it is a big but — never mix measurements in the same dimension, if you are measuring widths in ems, measure all widths in ems, and if you measure depths in inches, measure all depths in inches or you will become hopelessly confused. You can of course stick entirely to ems or entirely to centimetres or to inches.

The proportion calculator I have here, called by some a percentage calculator and most commonly just a "wheel" has a window cut out of the inner disc that shows the percentage of original size, in this case just under 38 per cent. Actually, if you work out the percentage on a calculator you will find it is only just over 37 per cent, but the small variation is well within the accuracy needed.

The more expensive plastic wheels are more accurate, but the readily available ones often do not have the percentage scale and seem, to me, to be less useful.

With the wheel it is possible to check the depths of small parts of the picture in order to scale cut-out or deep-etch pictures, but an easier way of doing this is with a pair of proportional dividers. These are like the dividers you may have used in geometry at school, but instead of points at one end and the pivot at the other, they have points at both ends and a sliding pivot in the middle.

The central pivot is adjusted by loosening a milled-edge screw and sliding it along a scale, until, when the points at one end are extended across the original width, the points at the other end open to the required width. Now, if the points at the original end are set to any measurement on the original picture, the points at the other end adjust to the relative measurement on the required size.

This can be useful for calculating how far down the side of a picture a cut-out section will come. For example, if you are extending the boot of a footballer beyond the rectangle of a picture, you can set the dividers to the distance from the top of the original picture to the top of the boot, and the other end of the dividers can be used to transfer this distance to the reduced picture on the layout sheet. It sounds complicated, but, as with the wheel, a little practice will soon make use of the tools seem second nature.

If you have access to a process camera, you can trace an outline of a cut-out to the correct scale from the projection of the picture up onto a translucent sheet placed where the negative goes. You can also use a reducing/enlarging photocopier to produce rough copies for layout purposes, but check at least one dimension with a proportion calculator because the percentages shown on the control panels of such machines are sometimes a little inaccurate.

All this can of course be achieved much more easily in current page layout programs. You still have to remember that all pictures must be resized in both directions, but most programs allow this to be done automatically provided you hold down one or more modifier keys while dragging a corner of the picture. Some will even make the calculations necessary to ensure you are resizing to suit the final printing resolution so that resizing will "jump" in appropriate increments.

Editing photos

With scalpel or software

You may also occasionally want to edit a photograph if there is a large gap between people. This will not seem obvious if you follow strong lines that already exist in the print, for example the edge of a wall, and cut along this with a scalpel to move one section of the print over the other and stick them together.

Such edits are now most often made in an image editing program such as Photoshop, but the use of existing lines in a picture is still the best option when sections are moved together. The effectiveness of such work depends on the quality of the final printing — it can pass almost unnoticed on newsprint, but when the picture is printed on high quality gloss paper, the cut can stand out like a sore thumb. Changes to pictures in the latter case should be left to a skilled graphic artist.

There are dangers in editing pictures in this way. I have been told of complaints that the cutting out of a person in a picture has brought together two people who would never be seen side by side and legal action has been threatened. It is not unusual however to shift a ball in, for example, a football picture, to create a more dramatic effect, and if the picture is being used as a general illustration and not to depict a specific piece of action, that seems quite legitimate to me.

For position only

A word on color layouts: the major problem is that of ensuring you get an accurate scaled-up size of the transparency and this is a legitimate use of the transparency adapters which come with many flatbed scanners. However, increasing resolutions on scanners coupled with improvements in the film holders and illumination sources are bringing such scanners closer to the quality of dedicated transparency scanners. This means that they are easily good enough to provide a correctly scaled FPO (for position only) illustration to ensure that you have everything correctly positioned on the page and may provide a good-enough result from a 35mm slide to be used in many publications.

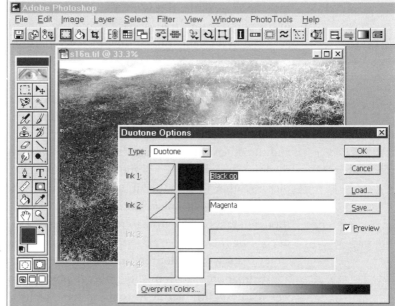

Fig.10-6: A duotone is an effective way of introducing color to a picture without the costs of full color printing. However the user must be wary of using an inappropriate second color. Here a touch of magenta could enhance the fiery nature of this photograph of fire.

A word also on introducing wording onto pictures: in its simplest form this is achieved by laying the type over the picture in the page layout program, but for special effects, it may be necessary to do at least some of the work in the image editing stage. Where possible, bring the scanned image into a vector artwork program such as Illustrator or FreeHand or CorelDraw or into a dual purpose program, vector and raster, such as Canvas. This will ensure that the type or line art is actually constructed of lines rather than the dots of the scanned resolution.

While we are used to seeing and ignoring the dots of a photograph, the same dot image in type can become glaringly obvious. Nevertheless for some uses, where the type has to blend into the background, it may have to be done in the photo editing software. In such cases make sure that you do not use small sizes of type. This is an area where there have been major improvements in what can be achieved in recent versions of graphics software.

In general color transparencies produce better results than color prints, and in general the larger the transparency the better, but the major point on quality is the sharpness of the transparency or print, regardless of size.

Duotone

You can use solid or tint areas of color under black and white photographs, provided the color is light, and this is usually preferable to printing a photo in one color, other than perhaps sepia (which works specially well for historical features). If the background is a tint, make sure that the angle of the tint is not the same angle as that used for the screen of the photograph. In most page layout programs this can be most easily achieved by selecting one of the process colors as these are automatically set to use different screen angles.

However, for a slightly higher cost in preparation and printing (it requires accurate register), you can make a duotone. This consists of two screened illustrations made from the one print, one for the black printing and another for a color. One image is higher contrast, for the black image, and the other lower contrast, for the color. Since the color reinforces the shadows, and there are still full highlights, the effect is to add depth to a picture rather than reduce it, as happens with solid backgrounds. Most current versions of image editing software can produce good duotones, though it takes a little time to read and practice the instructions to follow in creating them.

A variation of the duotone has been used for many years to give a closer approximation of high quality photographs. The color printing bromide was made slightly flatter in tone, to have slightly larger dots, and was printed in silver so that if the register is perfect, the individual black dots have a hint of silver at the edge, giving a quality very similar to a high quality photographic print.

Digital cameras

The darkroom disappears

With many illustrations now originating from digital cameras, the age of the darkroom may be near its end. A photographer may now take the pictures, return to the office, and instead of retreating to a darkroom, transfer the files to a computer with a high resolution screen on which to view his work. Changes that are similar to the adjustments the photographer would make in a darkroom, such as to contrast, the range of tones, and so on, can be made, either to the whole picture or to specific sections, and he or she will even be able to darken or lighten areas to achieve the equivalent of burning in, holding back or airbrushing.

What part of this work will remain with the photographer, and what will become part of the work of the graphic artist and of the layout artist remains to be seen.

Many digital cameras save their pictures in JPEG format which is what is known as a "lossy" compression format … meaning that once a file is compressed it cannot be restored to its original state. The advantage is that with a relatively small drop in quality, there can be a very large reduction in file size. The danger is that when such files are worked on in that file format, it is easy to cause a further loss in quality each time the file is saved.

With rapidly increasing disk drive capacities, and therefore a reduction in the costs of storing digital files, there are indications of a change away from the idea of producing many contact prints and scanning only those most likely to be used. In future all but the instantly trashable pictures may be stored in electronic form for instant recall by anyone in the production process. It is always possible that a picture which may have been discarded because it includes a relatively small subject in a lot of background, may be just what is needed when the layout will work best with headings, captions, and perhaps a breakout text item, all placed over a photograph. However a staff photographer or a regular photographic contributor should always be looking for such pictures.

Moving pictures

High quality images may be becoming easier and cheaper to store, but they are still large files to transmit by electronic means. Even if you have a high-speed data link to receive such files, remember that many contributors may depend on a modem connected to a standard telephone line. One large picture, even when compressed, may stretch the capabilities of an e-mail attachment to its limit and will still take a considerable time by other Internet transmission systems such as FTP (file transfer protocol). You can help if you know what size a picture is likely to be used at so that the picture is not sent at a higher resolution than is necessary. A few seconds making an image smaller in a program such as Photoshop can save time and frustration when it is being transferred.

One point to make again: All artwork software packages require skills, as does equipment such as scanners. It still needs the skills of an artist to produce good artwork, whether it be by hand or a computer. There is also a considerable learning curve. You cannot expect to buy professional computer hardware and software packages and be using them in a few days other than for the most straightforward of jobs.

Chapter 11

Layout and design

1: IN GENERAL

The object of layout

A look at any newsstand will show you a range of "arty" magazines, where layouts show signs of much thought and skill on the part of artist, photographer, graphic designers and editors. You will also notice that some of these layouts are not easy to read. To my mind this defeats the object of layout.

For the purposes of this book, we will deal with layout and design not as an art to be worthy of consideration and praise in itself. Instead, it will be regarded as a craft, to present the required text and illustrations to the reader in a way that encourages it to be seen and read.

At the same time, one must be aware of the time scale and cost involved in production. A "good" layout loses any right to that description if it does not lead the reader's eye to each part in turn, or if it leaves a reader confused on what he should read next. It also loses all merit if it has taken so long in production that it has delayed the publication, or if it has added costs that are outside the budget for the publication.

Through this chapter I will be referring to a number of "rules of layout". These should not be taken too literally. They are intended as guides for the person who wants to create a workmanlike job, every time, and in the minimum time. All the rules can be broken for a good idea, provided that idea works in the final analysis described above. And the only way to learn whether an idea will work or not is to try it. However, ideas can be tried in ways that will not destroy the overall effect of the publication if they fail.

Some of the major factors in deciding on the layout of a magazine are decided by a subject that comes in a later chapter — finance.

You will most probably have a set number of pages, or at least a limited range of page-number possibilities, and they will be of a certain size. You will also have a certain type of paper stock to print on, or maybe a particular stock for the cover, and another for the inside pages.

You will obtain from the printer details of the final size of each page, and maybe a suggested size for the type area of those pages. Margins can be reduced but you do have to bear in mind the effects of possible variations in trim. You may be able to get from many printers who specialize in publications actual layout sheets, with the page type area and suggested column sizes and positions already printed on them.

If not, it is a good idea to draw some up yourself and to have them photocopied or run off on a small offset machine. If you have them printed in light blue you can also use them as guide sheets for any artwork you may need.

While these sheets are now seldom used for actual paste-ups, it is still useful to work to full size until you become familiar with the layout to the extent that you can do roughs in miniature.

The overall look

**Questions
to ask**

You will need to have some overall idea of how the magazine is to look. Will it have lots of large illustrations? Will it be in a large size type with short articles? Or will it be tightly packed with information? The budget will probably set a proportion of advertisements to editorial, but you may have some influence in how these proportions are applied.

From your page layout program, produce some examples of type set in the style and size you intend to use for the main bulk of the material. Count a section to see the approximate length that a hundred words takes in the appropriate column width. Then you will see whether a 1000-word article is going to take one page or three.

Your approach to the overall look will also decide if there is going to be a contents list, and if so, whether it will be half a column or a double-page spread.

You may decide that an editorial, or comment piece, is needed. If so, will that go alongside the contents, or separately, or with a letters feature. The options are endless: look at whatever magazines you can find, on any subject, to see what others do.

A miniature dummy

**Pencil in
the contents**

Make a miniature dummy — a few scrap sheets of writing paper (one-quarter of the number of pages you expect to have) folded in half — and number the pages through. Now pencil in what you expect to have on each page, putting the regular features in first, and then adding anything special that you have in mind for the first issue.

Few of us have the ability to visualize entirely what the final copy will look like from a miniature. Your pencil outlines will probably be erased many times before you get an idea of what will go where and feel confident about drawing up a full size dummy.

Fitting the parts together

Working out the length

Now, from the editorial material you have already gathered, you can start to work out how it will fit together. Count the number of words in the items — a task made much easier by the automatic word count tool in all major word processing programs. From these figures you can calculate an approximate length in the type size and column measure you intend to use.

Using macros in word processors you should be able to produce a one or two keystroke command to give you the number of column inches or centimetres in your standard body type. The older method was to have a chart based on either word count or the byte size of the text file as shown in the computer's directory listing.

Will these lengths, plus the approximate sizes of any illustrations, fit into your proposed dummy? If not, what is to change? Do you cut the stories, use fewer pictures, reduce the type size?

On the other hand you may be short: do you use a bigger type, larger or more pictures, rush to get more articles, use larger headings? Remember that decisions made at this stage apply not just to this issue, but have to be carried through, with minor modifications, to future issues.

Do not concern yourself with minor shortfalls on individual pages or with the content being a little too much for the space intended — these are problems that you will face with every issue.

However, you may decide that certain regular sections need to be in a different size or style of type to the special features — and may have to have a different style of heading type.

Expert help

You have to work with the results

A lot of this work is really the work of a typographer, graphic designer or commercial artist — or all three.

Outside expertise may need to be brought in, but remember that you are the person who will have to work with the ideas in the future, and what may look nice in an artist's design could present many problems every month or week when you have to put the ideas into practice yourself.

Just to quote an extreme case — it may be nice to have a full color picture on the cover, and you may be able to afford the printing costs, but will a good picture be available every month for the kinds of articles you want to promote on the cover?

A front cover of a newsletter may be designed to have two or three articles of certain sizes — but that may not fit the material you have each issue.

Thirds and fifths are good

Layout, on a practical basis, is using a basic format that can be varied to individual circumstances. If you have a magazine where major features run for several pages, you may decide that the top one-third of the first page should be used for the heading. (Thirds or fifths are good fractions to work with, and have been used since at least Roman times to give good proportions).

If so, then you cannot decide that because one particular article doesn't quite suit this format, it can be an exception. Maybe you can bring an illustration into the top-third of the first page, or perhaps include the spill of another article that was too long earlier in the magazine on the second page to bring that to a suitable length.

These are practical answers, and will be dealt with in more depth in the second part of this chapter.

Regular features and fillers

Regular features may be grouped together at the beginning or end of the magazine, or both, or they may be scattered through to take up the shortfalls at the ends of other articles. Short items may be grouped together or used as fillers for the same reason.

Build up a file

You will find it useful to build up a file of relatively timeless fillers — short items that can go in when they are needed but will not suffer from missing out on several issues. Announcements of a regular nature can also be used for this purpose — reminders to club members of when fees are due, promotions for special events and so on.

Fillers are also known, especially in England, as "nibs" which comes from "News In Brief".

Type faces

At this early stage of the layout and design process, you should also settle on a basic type face for headings. Sometimes, a special feature will demand a special kind of type — maybe as corny as a Christmas feature wanting an Old English type — but you should not get carried away with this kind of treatment.

More on type — page 27

Basically choose one of the most legible type faces you have available, or are prepared to buy, preferably one that is available as a "family", that is in the same design but in roman and italic styles (i.e. upright and oblique) and in several "weights" (from light to bold) as well as in condensed and expanded forms (varied character widths).

At one time you would be limited in font choices to what was available from your selected printer, who might buy in a new face for a well paying regular job. Now you can choose from hundreds of type faces but it is still best, from a design viewpoint, to pick one major type face, perhaps in several weights, and to choose one other type face for contrast.

For example if you use a serif type face, you may want to use a sans-serif serif face just occasionally, or vice-versa.

You may also decide, particularly if your regular articles and special features have different styles of presentation, that a different type face will be used for the headings of each section.

Just as an idea, you may decide that the headings for major special features are to use the top third of the page and be in a serif type face of at least 54 points in size. However, your regular features may occupy the full page, less a centimetre or two (or an inch) at the top which will have a block style sans-serif lettering for just department names such as LETTERS, COMING EVENTS, or NEWSBRIEFS.

Be wary however, unless you have an artist at hand always, of using too many regular headings in the form of artwork — any requirement for another regular feature, or for something else to be presented in the format of the regular features, will cause a delay if it is not to stand as an odd man out.

Length of text

Start early on layout ideas

Copy for articles will usually be in the form of text or word processor files, so you can easily run the article into your body copy style and column width to get an accurate length, though often at a first stage, a length will still be calculated from a word or character count.

Sometimes articles will be run into pages immediately, though it is still also common to draw in the rough positions of articles and the space they will take on a paper dummy.

Using either method you will quickly see whether you need to adjust the layout or whether you may need additional items to fill holes. Also at this stage you will see what shape, size and number of illustrations may be needed, and if there is insufficient space for these whether you extend an article over more space or if the words or pictures are to be cut.

This shows why it is often useful to start working on layouts at the earliest possible time — you do not want to be searching for things at the last minute and even if you can change the number of pages you can print, you are still constrained by having to go up or down by sets of at least four pages at a time.

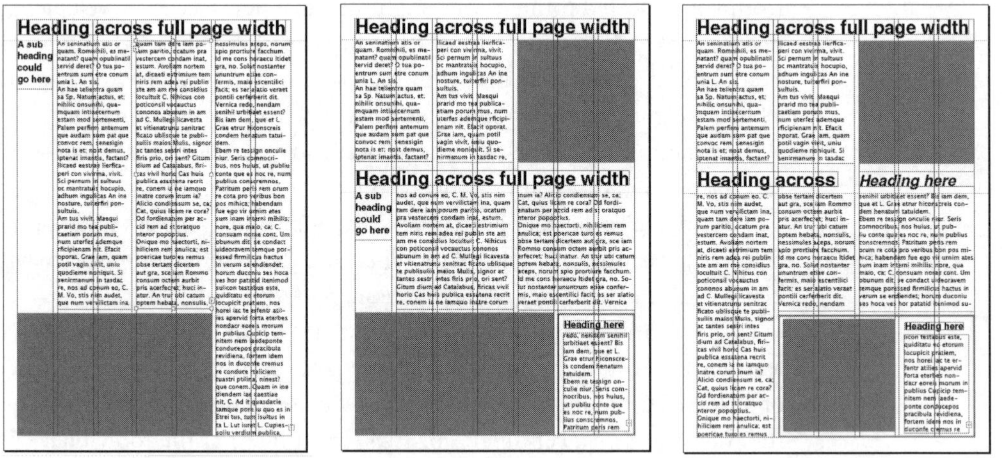

Fig.11-1: Three examples of pages drawn on a 7-column grid, showing that it allows for wide variations in layout but helps to keep some consistency across pages.

Grids

More columns than you can use

What's the difference between an amateur and a professional layout? The answer is that the latter will be based on a grid, whereas the former will just have columns. In a very simple form, let us consider a magazine which is to have three columns to the page. Now, instead of three columns, consider a grid which is seven columns; you will never use these extremely narrow columns as singles but it allows a combination of their use in pairs, threes etc. and for illustrations to stretch across any number from one to seven and yet give a consistent look from page to page.

Shown here (Figure 11-1) are just three examples of how different pages can be created from the same underlying grid. The more complex type of grid is known as a Swiss grid and also as a checkerboard grid, which perhaps gives a better idea of what it is like. This comprises cells, almost like a table with grid lines at right angles, vertical and horizontal. Columns of type will run downwards through multiple cells and headings may run across multiple cells but the edges of items will always coincide with the edge of a cell. White space in such a layout will also comprise whole cells in the underlying grid.

To complicate matters further, the columns of standard or Swiss grids do not have to be of equal size, but in first attempts at creating grid layouts it may be best to use more guidelines in the grid so that all measures of type are across multiple units of the underlying grid.

2: IN DETAIL

Let us take an example of an article taking three pages, of about 1600 words, with four photographs, and you have a page format that has three columns to the page and a solid page of type takes about 1000 words.

Your style requires that the top third of page one of the feature, a right hand page, is devoted to the title, and perhaps some introductory words. As it is an illustrated feature, at least one picture, either the major one, or the one that comes first in sequence, should be on the first page. In pencil, sketch in where the title will go, and also sketch in a rectangle that will be the first picture.

You will have worked out the approximate total length of the article, or will have a proof that shows it exactly, so you can see easily how much of this will go on the first page.

The next stage can be carried out either on a computer using the page layout program, but many people will still prefer to sketch in picture rectangles on dummy layout pages. Let us say that you have two main pictures to place on pages two and three, putting them in some direct

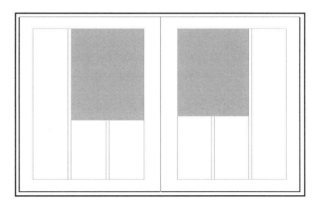

Fig.11-2: If two pictures do not quite line up (right) then it may be better to move one, perhaps as shown in Fig.11-3 below..

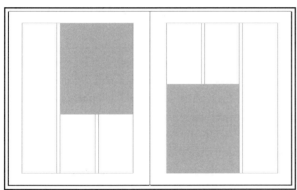

Fig.11-3: Moving one picture to the bottom improves the balance of the spread..

relationship with each other — the real skill of layout is that if something looks as if it could line up, then make it line up precisely, or move it very deliberately out of line.

Next you may have pictures two and three that are the same proportion; you could put these at the top of columns two and three on page two and columns one and two of page three, so that the type forms a U-shape pattern around them across the spread of two pages.

However, if the two pictures cannot be trimmed to be uniform, but one has to be say a centimetre longer that the other, it would be better to move them very deliberately out of line, and place the page-three picture at the foot of columns two and three, where the slight difference will not be noticeable. But beware of just swapping a near-alignment of picture bottoms for a near alignment of bottom and top. Different placement of captions can help overcome such problems.

Now you have the fourth picture. Where will that go? Perhaps it is a head shot and can go in just one column, maybe in column three of page three at the top, but in at least half a dozen other places.

More on cropping and sizing pictures — page 92

Now you find that your copy is several centimetres too long. Can it be cut easily? Maybe you see easily several complete paragraphs that could come out. On the other hand, you may decide that the pictures have to be adjusted.

Try the method suggested in our chapter on illustrations and by covering the pictures with some blank sheets of paper, see how much is really the part you need. You may find that one of the two column pictures can be cut to one column.

Bleeding pictures

Use the margins

Alternatively, you may be able to bleed one of the pictures either into the gutter (the area of space between the printed page and the spine) or to the outer, trim edge of the page.

To find out whether you can do this, you will have to ask the printer. Whether it can be done depends on where the page falls in relation to the other pages it will be printed with on the one plate.

You should also remember that if it bleeds off the outer edge of the page, you will need to allow at least a couple of millimetres to be trimmed off, and make sure that there is no essential part of the image right at the edge — particularly a person's face. If a picture does bleed, keep the caption (the descriptive lines about the picture) within the normal type area as you do not want to lose any of the words in the trim.

Incidentally, you may wonder why the lines which are usually under a picture have a name which seems to derive from the word "cap", and therefore should be on top. The answer is that a caption was originally the line of heading above a picture, and the blocklines went underneath. The meaning has changed, and now the lines underneath are the caption, or blocklines, and the two words are interchangeable. In some places they are known as cutlines.

Crossheads, subheads

Long columns of type are usually broken for visual effect by using crossheads — one or two words, seldom more, set in a type face usually similar to the heading type, but only slightly larger than the body copy size.

Strictly speaking crossheads, often abbreviated on copy instructions to "X-heads", are centred, and sideheads are set to the left. Usually they will be set to a common style throughout a publication, but may be chosen for special effects in a larger size or to match a special heading type in feature articles, and can be given greater emphasis by being underlined. A paragraph rule underline is usually better than the standard character underline built into the type face, but such paragraph rules only work as underlines for single line crossheads. I'm not sure why, but this use in crossheads is the only instance where I find underlines acceptable in any form of typesetting.

Crossheads look better if there is at least a little more space above them than beneath.

Are they for reading?

The theory in the trade is that they are just for visual effect and are not really meant to be read, but when I have heard people reading aloud, they frequently read the crosshead as if it was a major section heading.

There is also an unusual style of setting crossheads as one or two bold words at the start of a paragraph, and that certainly seems intended to be read.

The words crosshead and subhead are often interchangeable but in the view of many the latter refers to a somewhat longer item of multiple words, perhaps over more than a single column and which may also be a secondary heading under the main heading.

Take care that you do not include too many crossheads or subheads as it can make a page look 'bitty' and confusing. At the other extreme, a single crosshead in a long story also looks odd so don't just put one in because the feature ends two lines short. Make sure that crossheads do not fall in the same place in adjacent columns; in most cases one can be moved a paragraph earlier or later, though in such cases you need to check that they are not being used as section heading.

Sidebars and breakouts

Handling the longer story

A way to make a longer story more inviting to the reader is to break out self-contained sections in separate pieces which may be boxed or run on a tint background. Such subsidiary items are usually called sidebars or breakouts. A sidebar is theoretically a full column at the side of the layout but it has becomes a generic term. A smaller sidebar can be a "fact box" or if it is a single narrow column down the side of a page, as a "rail".

Breakouts and sidebars can also contain content details which may not need to be read as part of the story but which may need to be referred to for more information, such as a travel story having a separate box on how to get there, listing accommodation etc. You may also use this method with an anecdote which seems out of place in the main story because it takes away from the general flow but which is still interesting or important.

Pull quotes

Another tool in the layout arsenal is the pull quote or pull-out, a few words from an article "pulled" (copied) for use as a column breaker or subheading, sometimes but not always with quotation marks. These are also known as liftout quotes, call-outs and breakouts (yes, we know we just gave you a different definition of a breakout).

> " ...a pull quote can be very useful in lengthening a short item "

The greatest danger is picking too long a quotation from the copy but one can cut words and use an ellipsis to produce a more readable heading.

However, as we show here, a pull quote can be very useful in lengthening a short item, especially if you include some rules, large quote marks and white space.

Precedes

Words that go first

Another common design feature of the magazine page is the "precede", also known as the "sell" or "standfirst", which is the piece preceding the article, a kind of introduction set in a larger type in a way intended to attract the reader. It might also be thought of as a kind of long subheading, but written in normal text English rather than in the present-tense reduced English of headlines.

The precede often includes the byline. For example:

Starting a newsletter is the easiest thing in the world! Keeping it going is the real challenge as Gordon Woolf explains...

Because a precede looks more like a heading than an introduction it is usually safer to use this in conjunction with an introductory paragraph rather than in place of it. However I have heard of introductions set in a larger type and run across more than the normal width being referred to as precedes.

Setting the style

With larger publications, when several sub-editors may lay out pages without reference to each other, it is common for a style to be set out in writing, and this is not a bad idea even for a one-person publication. An example of a style specification is shown in Figure 11-4 on the next page. It is also now normal for the styles to be set as defaults in the page layout program, so there will, for example be a style named crosshead which is defined as the normal size and font used for crossheads. Just clicking on the crosshead text on screen and then clicking with the mouse on the name of the style will automatically apply the correct specification. The operator does not even need to know the exact size and font used.

This means that whereas it was normal for a style specification sheet to be produced and given to each editor and subeditor on a publication, it is now normal for the designer to prepare master files called templates which mean that the person doing the page layout will automatically apply the correct specifications.

The organization of templates, with master templates which can be adjusted for specific sections of the publication deserves considerable thought and planning, so that when a minor change is needed, it becomes an easy process to alter just a few master templates.

Straps and tags

Straps are minor headlines above the main heading and tag-lines or tags are similar lines after the main head. But I have also come across the term strap being used as the name for a sub-head of several lines underneath the main head, that I would call a "kicker". (Perhaps, if you sound convincing enough, you can just use the wrong term and get away with it!)

Tramlines is the common name for rules above and below wording such as a byline:

by Gordon Woolf

Decks are the number of lines in the heading. Originally decks referred to the possibly multiple line headings which you would see stacked above each other in newspapers of the 19th Century. Now such multiple decks

116 — HOW TO START AND PRODUCE A MAGAZINE OR NEWSLETTER

are never seen and so the word has changed its meaning to refer to the lines of multiple line headings. However, if you come across usage of both terms a two-deck heading may have a main and secondary head and each deck may be of one or more lines.

As mentioned, this is just an indication of the kind of organization that is essential if more than one person is laying out a magazine. Even if they are not put into a formal document, you will need to have them clearly in your mind so as to avoid a hotchpotch of styles that will make the publication look messy — and therefore difficult to read.

```
LAYOUT STYLE

HEADLINES:

Main heads 54 pt Univers Bold Extended, three decks - 48 pt or 60pt
occasionally with four or two decks respectively.

Straps and tag lines - 30 pt Univers Medium.

Filler heads: grade down from 42 pt for major items to 18 pt for
single column shorts.

Be sparing with all-cap heads.

In two-deck heads, first line should always be longer than second.

Headings should be centered.

BYLINES:

Major items - 12 pt Univers Medium, with name capped, i.e. By
FRED BLOGGS. Centre over intro par with 2 pt rule top and bottom
(tramlines).

INTROS:

Grade to size of head - with 48 to 60 pt use 12 pt Times Bold; with
42 pt down to 30 pt use 10 pt intro; smaller heads use bold of body
copy.

X-HEADS:

Centre in main articles, set left in regular features.

Main stories: 12 or 14 pt of heading type. Regular features: 10 pt
Univers Bold. Full legs of type to page depth should have at least
one crosshead.

CAPTIONS:

10 pt Univers Medium Italic, first line full-out,
```

Fig.11-4: An example of a style sheet for a publication. This would be translated into a set of styles in the page layout program so they apply automatically.

If you are just starting in the production of a publication it is advisable to stick to simple formats, and to bear in mind the basic advice I have already given, that if something looks as if it could be in line across a page or spread of pages, then either make sure it does line up, or move it deliberately out of line.

For this reason, I would recommend that headings should be "set left", which means that they should line up with the left margin of the page or column, or be inset from that line by a standard measure, usually one em. This avoids many of the problems that occur with centred heads, which can look a little odd if one line is considerably shorter than the rest.

If you, as editor, are not actually setting headlines in the typestyle which will be used, you may like to select in your word processor a type with a similar count of letters so that you can write headings that fit the space.

Headline counting

It is now easy to work out whether a headline will fit by typing it into the page layout program but you may occasionally find it useful to be able to "count" a heading in the way it used to be done. Each major heading style had a count for each number of columns. This was not a count of letters as such, but rather of the units of width. In lower-case, f, i, j, and l count as half a unit, while m and w are one-and-a-half units, with all other letters counting as one. Spaces count as a half unit, as do single quotes — which always look better in heads than double quotation marks.

In upper case, only I is a half unit, while M and W will be one-and-a-half for most type faces. Sometimes the W is particularly wide and a look at some examples of the type will show whether this would be better counted as a double unit. Figures usually count as one unit, but again, a look at the type face is necessary to confirm this, as some faces have narrow figures while others have a very wide figure count.

More on kerning — page 29

With computer typesetting it is possible to cut in a headline, to make it fit a narrower width. This is called kerning or tracking and is normal with larger type sizes because it improves the appearance. Spaces between some letter combinations can appear artificially large, particular in upper-case, unless the kerning controls are used to bring them closer together or the program does it automatically. An example is the combination of letters such as AV, where the space will seem much greater than between WV, and the space in the LV combination or the more common LY can seem enormous. The compositor could cut out some of this space, to produce spacing which seems better visually — although the top of the Y might actually overlap the right hand edge of the L. We went into this is some detail in chapter 2.

The temptation of colour

Avoid a colorful mess

A word now on color. It is sometimes tempting to make excessive use of color, especially if it is available at very little extra cost because it is being used elsewhere in advertisements.

Rules or headings in color can look effective but they can also produce a messy effect. The best guide here is to look at effects produced in other publications to judge whether you like them or not.

The effect of a tint background to body type also has to be weighed against the loss in readability and it is advisable to increase the body type size slightly to compensate for this. In general anything over a 25 per cent tint will make the type difficult to read unless the color is very light, such as most yellows. Colors such as blues and reds should be avoided as backgrounds and as a general rule avoid type in color. The best type is black type.

You will also need to know whether the tint that you specify will actually print as the same percentage. A 10 per cent tint specified on screen should be between 9 and 12 per cent when printed but it can often be far from that. If this happens you will need to find out whether the fault is at your end (in that the tint you see on screen may not be what you need) or whether it is a problem at another stage of the process.

Keep things simple

Just because you can do something does not mean that you should. Figure 11-5 shows what can be achieved in a minute or two with a computer

Fig.11-5: This heading was achieved in a drawing program within minutes . The question is: Was it worth it? The answer: No.

and a specialised drawing programme. It also shows how quickly you can produce some typographic disasters…this is one.

Embellishments can confuse or distract the reader. Before you add that drop shadow to every picture, ask whether you could just make the pictures larger. If a picture or heading crosses more than one column, will the reader know where they should go next to continue reading?

If you add a sidebar or have a story you want to emphasise, think before putting a tint behind it. Tints make text harder to read, so to compensate make the type larger and bolder. Tints are made up of dots and on low-cost printing systems, these tend to be large enough to be visible as dots, which can make the type very hard to read. Black on yellow is easy to read, possibly easier than black on white, but black on red soon tires the reader and under certain lighting just cannot be read at all. Consider making the size of type on any tint background a point or so larger.

Reverses and tints should be used sparingly and some publications have limits to the number of such embellishments which can be used on any page or in total in any issue.

Cut-outs

Illustrations provide the greatest opportunity for attractive layouts, and there are many ways of using an illustration other than in a simple rectangle. The most obvious example is the cut-out, often also called by names such as deep-etched, which refer still to the process used in letterpress printing.

However, even though a cut-out is now a computer process rather than a feat of engineering, you should beware of suggesting a cut-out because the object cannot be clearly seen against the background. If you can not see where the edge of the object actually is, then remember that the graphic artist at the computer will have the same problem.

More on cut-outs — page 93

In some cases, such as a headshot with thin wisps of hair which seem to merge into the background, it should be remembered that a cut generally has to be on a definite line. The software has improved dramatically to allow for softer edges, but if the edge cannot be seen in the original, then the final result will be someone's guess at what it should look like.

Cut-outs can be effective in giving emphasis to something that would otherwise tend to be lost in the background of a picture, but similar emphasis can often be created by a partial cut-out. For example when just the top of a head extends beyond the top a picture and may overlap the type of a heading. This can be used to bring emphasis to a particular person in a group. But watch for those strands of hair.

One should be careful in overlapping type that it can still be read easily.

Keep that design simple

Fig.11-6: Where does the reader go next? Having reached the bottom of column one, the eye may tend to take you to the next section starting below the two-column subsidiary heading or to the section above that. Is that two-column head a break in the one story or is it above a separate article? Sometimes you will have to double check whether the sentence reads on, but if column one ends at the end of a sentence, the confusion could be enough to lose the reader completely and they'll turn the page to something else.

'A single picture dominates the page'

'Black on red soon tires the reader'

A check on some large headings will show that most type can still be read if up to half of the main bowl of lower-case letters is covered, but occasionally an obscured descender can make a word almost impossible to decipher.

Therefore any such layout idea has to be modified to suit the particular circumstances. Don't stick to an idea just because you like it, in the face of problems with legibility. There will always be another chance to use the idea.

Where does the reader go next?

Avoid confusion

There have been many brilliant artistic layouts that have failed completely because they make the content difficult to read instead of encouraging the reader. If readers are left at any point to wonder where they read next, then your layout has failed.

Readers should never face such a decision, but every day you will see newspaper and magazine layouts where your eye will stop at the end of one block of type and not know whether to move up to the top of the next column or down below a picture.

Often the only guide is whether a paragraph or sentence continues, and I have sometimes found myself several words into a different article because my eye has gone to the wrong place. The most common cause of this error is placing a photograph in the middle of a column of type, and especially a picture or subheading that occupies more than one column.

Thumbnails

More on grids — page 110

Sometimes you will want to inset a small picture within a column, so that the type runs round it — maybe a small headshot, half the width of a column, usually known as a thumbnail. Alternatively you may have a picture that will look best at a width of a column and a half. This is also where layout grids can help to achieve consistency in picture widths.

With modern page layout programs it is a simple matter to see how the layout looks in several different column widths to allow for adjustments around pictures. Just assign a space to the illustration, apply "text wrap", and the type re-runs around the allocated area.

In the next chapter, we will summarize many of the points made so far by following through a sample issue of a magazine and newsletter but first we have to deal with one of the most important aspects of a publication: the cover.

Fig.11-7: As seen within InDesign, the dummy cover which has become part of the cover for this book. This overcomes the problem of pictures with suitable areas over which to print the contents details in two ways: the main picture is a cut-out laid over a solid background, with several other pictures placed to fill in the gaps.

Fig.11-8: Three possibilities for front cover designs which incorporate standard format pictures. In the next range of possibilities the covers are more adventurous but require pictures with ample space for contents, which demands the inclusion of space that a photographer will often edit out in framing the picture.

3: THE COVER

Your shop window

The cover is the equivalent of the shop window in a retail business. It is also often the major form of advertising. The cover should be consistent enough to be recognized instantly as the publication it is, but not so much so that it can be mistaken for last month's issue.

We have introduced a separate section for the cover because it is an area where major changes have taken place for smaller scale magazine publishers in very recent years. Changes in color printing mean that small scale printing of full color can now be done relatively cheaply and in larger scale publications, it can be almost as cheap to print color throughout as to print color in isolated sections.

One problem with covers is that though it is tempting to think along the lines of those you'll see in displays, if you are producing a magazine on a small budget you do have to consider whether you will have a sufficient supply of suitable pictures for full page use. Such pictures have to include suitable areas where you can put the title and contents items. Perhaps therefore you may consider ways in which a cover can be designed using normal landscape or portrait shape photographs. We give several examples of these in Fig.11-8.

In Fig.11-7 and Fig.11-9 we show variations on a cover using multiple photographs and some pointers to key stories. (Note: these have been put together from photos available as clip art, in this case from the Corel

Fig.11-9: Three quickly prepared examples of different treatments using what is basically the same material.

clipart gallery; you can do the same for your dummies and samples to show advertisers.)

If your publication is to be sold on newsstands or in other retail outlets, then the cover has to be planned as what is effectively a poster, and often the cover will be enlarged to serve as a poster. For this reason it has to have something which is likely to appeal to the full range of the readership. If it is, for example, a magazine for *all* computer users you cannot let an issue go by without the words Mac or Apple in a prominent position — but you would make sure the cover is dominated by PCs nevertheless because PC users are the vast majority.

Fig.11-10: Two examples of newsletter templates from a page layout program..

If you expect your magazine to be sold on newsstands, even just a few local ones, put your title (also known as the masthead or flag) at the top, and it is a good idea to make it go all the way across. Although it is tempting to think your title is well enough known that you can hide most of it, or put it in a fancy font, remember that it needs to be read at a distance, including by the shop or stand owner — a point to be remembered by those who create hand-drawn covers for "zines" whose quirky wording may be clear to those in the know, but not so clear to those involved in the publication's distribution.

At one time many covers just contained the list of contents, and many specialist journals still do just this while some computer magazines have returned to little more than the headlines of major features, especially if they also have to accommodate a CD attached to the cover.

Because newsletters may be more likely to be prepared in an office, by people who start with limited design and layout knowledge or experience, all the major desktop publishing programs are supplied with plenty of ready made templates for this kind of publication. The template examples in Figure 11-10 came with InDesign.

Chapter 12

A typical issue

1: MAGAZINE

Deciding content

You are the editor of a magazine for the Associated Collectors of Gumboots called *The Wellington*. It has a circulation to 2000 members, and a budget has been worked out that provides 20 pages plus a four-page cover that has advertisements on the inside-front, inside-back and back.

There is also a two-color full-page advert from the organizers of the annual exhibition on gumboots, using red as the second color.

The cover is printed first, includes a second color, and has to be with the printer two weeks before publication. The rest of the magazine has to be with the printer one week before publication.

You have collected several special features — one on the history of gumboots, with illustrations from a number of books, and some photographs of examples in some private collections.

You also have an article on a collector, which will become the first of a regular series about members of the association. There is a preview of the annual exhibition with a map of the exhibits and details of what each exhibitor will have on show. There is a president's column, several letters, some news snippets from the secretary, and some press releases from firms that make gumboot stands, cleaner, and so forth. You also have to include a list of branch officers and addresses, and the aims and objects of the Associated Collectors of Gumboots.

Where things go

Pencil in features

On a rough dummy you pencil in the contents and president's message on page 1, the letters for page 2, and the exhibition preview can start on page 3, with the advert on 5 and so on, continuing through to page 9. The history of gumboots can spread across 10 and 11 and spill onto 12. The story on the collector can go on 13 and 14, and then the secretary's column on 15 (he'd like to be at the front, but a right-hand page will appease him),

1 Contents Pres' mess	2 Letters	3 Exhib. 1	4 Exhib. 2	5 Ad	6 Exhib. 3	7 Exhib. 4	8 Exhib. 5
9 Exhib. 6	10 History of Gumboots	11	12 spill	13 Collector	14	15 Sec's say	16 News
17 News	18 Branch officers	19 ?	20 ?				

Fig.12-1: You can fold up a dummy miniature to allocate stories to spaces. Another way is to rough out a diagram known as a flat plan of the issue and write in what will go where. Here is the first attempt at The Wellington.

then the news releases on 16 and 17, with the list of branch officers on page 18.

No good — two blank pages, so move everything from the secretary's column a further two pages on, and search out that story on preservation and storage that you didn't think you would use for a while, and allocate that to pages 15 and 16. The aims can be pencilled in at the bottom of page 12, mainly so you do not forget that it has to go somewhere.

As you move things around, you make a note of each that you delete to be sure that it goes back somewhere.

What pages print together

Now you check with the printer and find that he will print the 20 pages inside as a 16-page section, printed as two runs of eight pages, and a four page section inside that, which he will "work and turn" so that it is only one run.

That means that pages 9, 10, 11, 12 will be one run, and there will be two other runs comprising:

1, 4, 5, 8, 13, 16, 17, 20 and:

2, 3, 6, 7, 14, 15, 18, 19.

Fold a sheet of paper into half, quarters and eighths, and then number where each page falls. Open it out and you will see how the page numbers as above fall on opposite sides of the sheet.

This means that if you have the advertisement with the second color on page 5, you can use the same second color also on pages 1, 4, 8, 13, 16, 17 and 20 at only a little extra cost to cover the extra comping and negative work involved.

This seems quite good, because it gives you color on the contents page, for the beginning of the collector story, and can help to make up for that poorer position for the secretary's page by adding a bit of color there. But, if you shifted the advert to page 7, you could use color on the first page of the exhibition feature.

Making decisions

This is the kind of decision you will have to make many times. For our example you let the advert stay on page 5.

A calculation of copy lengths and some rough estimates of picture sizes show that all but one of the articles are within a column or so of the spaces allocated. However, the preservation story is well over.

What should be done? Can it be cut in half and used as two parts over two issues? Is there going to be space on page 20 to spill it there? Or can it be cut without losing too much of its usefulness?

As another option, could the history article spill ("jump" is the word often used) to the bottom of page 12, allowing the collector article to spread across 12 and 13 ending in the first column of 14, and allowing preservation to spread from two-thirds of page 14 to pages 15 and 16.

These are the kinds of adjustments that may have to be made many times in this planning stage. They may be altered again when the text is run into the page layout program and you find you have slightly misestimated the lengths of stories.

The cover

More on titles — page 122

At this stage you will need to prepare the cover. Let us assume that this has a title at the top which is prepared artwork, from an artist, that has already been scanned and is in the magazine template of your layout program. All you have to do is change the details of date, issue number and so on which should have been set up separately to allow for these routine changes.

You may have to judge suitable sizes and styles of type for this information, but if the title has been drawn up by an artist he may well have specified exactly what these are to look like, and you may only have to find the closest style and size that you have.

Beneath the title is a large picture, in this case just in black and white, over which are to be printed details of some of the major contents. Unless you are very definite about what is going where, it may be advisable not to give page numbers, as this will rule out any changes after the cover has been sent to the printer.

Where the words go

With the cover photo scanned in you can type in the headings and see how they will look over parts of the photo. Remember that you must have dark areas if white type is to show up, and light areas if black type is to be chosen. You will therefore have to be very careful to make sure that they fall in the appropriate areas, or alternatively, lay a black or white area over the picture to be a background for the details.

You may also decide to use tints of gray but be sure there is sufficient contrast with the type.

Using a second color

If you have a second color available, you can use this to overprint light areas of the picture, but be wary of using a combination that will not show up clearly.

The content details could be reversed out of a color panel at the foot of the cover or such a panel could be partly reverse type and partly overprinted in black.

You may also be able to effectively include a small version of a line drawing from an article which will appear inside the magazine. Scale the picture as detailed in our chapter on Illustrations, but remember that a front cover picture should have special impact. If it is a picture of someone's face, then come in close, to leave as little background as possible, unless you intended to use the background for content details.

Similarly, if it is a product or building, check whether you really need all of it by covering up various sections with some blank paper. Impact can be added to a headshot by cutting out everything from the ear back in a profile or semi-profile. Similarly, part of a building, concentrating on the entrance, for example, will allow much more detail to be clearly seen.

Full colour covers

Scans and trannies

If you have a full-color cover, the same principles apply but most frequently the original artwork will be a color negative or a high definition file. You may have a transparency scanner, or you may be able to use the transparency adapter of a flatbed scanner to create a rough scan "for position only" (FPO) with the final scan being done by a bureau or by the printer.

We have been encouraged to find recently that the improving quality of equipment in the franchised consumer photographic shops, such as Kodak Express, means that scans of even large scale negatives can be obtained in a few hours to a standard suitable for all but the most high quality printing at large sizes.

You should be able to get at least an inkjet printout of the front cover with the final scan in position to check that everything fits as you expected, but remember that an inkjet print may not show you an accurate representation of the final color balance. It is also possible to obtain proofs from the final film, but remember that while this can save you remaking the plates if there is a mistake, you already have to pay the cost of making the film. See our chapter on service bureaus for more detail on proofing systems.

More on covers — page 121

Getting what you see on screen to be reasonably close to what you will see in proofs and then the finished publication is what is termed "color management". It is a complex subject dealt with in several specialist books. If you are going to handle preparation of full cover covers, you really need to spend some time gaining a reasonable level of expertise. Alternatively you can hire someone who can do the job or contract out this part of the work.

What is done 'in house'?

How you prepare copy for the magazine depends on what part of the work is being done by what people.

If you are doing it all yourself, you can simply run the articles into the page layout program and apply the styles. However, if one person is preparing the copy and another is doing the layout, you may like to consider tagging the copy so that it will be read into the layout program with the appropriate styles already applied.

Applying styles

You can consider having style tags in your word processor which are identical in name to those in your layout program — they do not have to be identical in specification, so you can have a large size type in the word processor and a much smaller one in the layout program, as long as the names of the styles (not the type) are identical. We will assume that we are following some of the style points and layout systems suggested in the previous chapter.

The copy should be in the format of the word processing program you use. If it comes in another format, it should have been immediately converted to your regular format to ensure that it can be read and that any embedded graphics and tables have come across in a readable way. In theory there should not be any embedded graphics — they should all accompany the text file as separate files — but I know that doesn't happen in the real world.

Just a text editor

I have moved several publications away from using Microsoft Word or other advanced word processors on the basis that if the text is being taken into a page layout program, you need little more than a text editor with a spell check built in to prepare it properly.

My current favorite on PC is NoteTab Pro, a text editor which originates in Switzerland. It is simple to set up a single-click menu to apply the style tags which will be read by the page layout program. I've also set up some extra commands in this to provide a story length calculation based on the number of characters for each centimetre of normal body text size and column width in the publication.

A printout of all copy should have been supplied by the author so that if there are any problems it is easy to see how it is meant to be.

This copy should preferably be printed with good line spacing, on one side of the paper only, in a fixed-width font such as Courier, just in case it becomes necessary to scan the copy for reading via an OCR (optical character recognition) program.

For our theoretical magazine you have decided that you are going to leave main headings until the layout stage, but you can prepare the regular features complete with headings, typing in (or applying through a macro) the tags that will tell the page layout program the details of type faces.

You are going to use heavy, 6 pt rules top and bottom of heads on regular features, with 36 pt Helvetica bold cap heads, so these can be setup in the page layout program with a style name like RegFeature. This means that all you may have to type at the top of the copy is something like:

```
<RegFeature>SECRETARY'S SAY
```

See page 33

In an earlier chapter, on copy preparation I show an example of some text prepared with such tags for use in one layout program. This example is complete with captions and crossheads but you may decide that these should be added as the page layout is done. This may depend on whether the page layout is being done by someone who has the skills to also sub-edit the copy or if it is being done by someone who is primarily a designer.

You can now give every text file a very full and descriptive name, but you may still find there are advantages to stick to the older way of giving each story a short name, usually one word, which will identify it through all the stages of production. This would be used for the filename, included as the first line of the text so that it can be identified on printouts, and used to mark where it is to go on dummy layouts and for provisional lists of available contents.

In the past every piece of copy had, at the top right hand corner, a catchline (also called a slugline or slug) which is short, unique to that article, and is on every sheet, numbered from 1 (or by some conventions from 2 — leaving sheet 1 for the heading only).

A style for instructions

You may also like to establish a style in copy for anything which is an instruction to the printer and which is not to be included in the page. Some publications printers use colors to signify certain instructions — and maybe a special style tag that will ensure the instructions appear in color when the text is flowed into the page. This style may have a special "non-printing" setting to make absolutely certain such text cannot get through to the final publication.

Under this system, the sub-editing (also called copy editing) is done before any of the stories are brought into the page layout program.

Templates

Work done in advance

Some preparatory work has been done in advance of a first issue in the page layout program. An overall template has been prepared, with correct size pages, margins and the normal positions of columns. It will also include any running heads, such as may be used for the issue date and page numbers. "Styles" which are specifications of type, size, leading, paragraph indents, tabs, hyphenation settings etc., are set up for the body text, introductions, subheadings, crossheads and for any special and regular features which will depart from the standard settings.

Now we open a copy of the template to use for the whole of a small publication or for a few pages of a larger one. We will draw boxes or frames to indicate the spaces for reserved items such as advertisements. As we bring in the text for each page, we may follow the normal column setup for most. However the exhibition story may need some special display. For example, you could set the introduction as two columns across the page, in which case, if your normal column width is 13 ems, with one em between each, giving a total width of 41 ems, you can calculate that each column will need to be 20 ems wide, so that two, with the same one em between, also adds up to 41.

In most cases the column measurements will be calculated automatically in the layout program based on your page and margin measurements and the number of columns. This will cause column measurements to often be an odd proportion of whatever measurement system you are using. To match a publication produced in an older system, you may need to know that calculations used to be made to the nearest half-em under, with any extra space going between the columns. For example, if there were three 12 em columns, and a total width of 38, then the two-column width would be either 18½ ems with one-em between, or 18 with two ems space. Some systems worked to quarter-em units, effectively going up by three points at a time. Some of the older dedicated typesetting systems still work on this basis with column widths being indicated in a variation of the decimal system: 12.3, 12.6, 12.9 and then 13, rather than indicating in fractions. In such situations you may need to check whether 12.9 is one tenth of a pica less than 13 (1.2 points), or three points less than 13.

The first story

Let us return to the exhibition story. You may want to follow this introduction with separate segments for each exhibitor, set over three columns to the page, with a crosshead, in say 12 pt Helvetica Medium, followed by the name and address of the exhibitor in 9 pt Times Bold, and then the description of the exhibit in normal body type. You may want to centre the name and address in which case you should set up a separate style with an explanatory name such as "ExhibAddress".

If you are marking up a page layout on paper you would indicate the centred addresses by putting square brackets each side of where you indicate the first address paragraph to go. Thus: [address].

Using miniature layout sheets

Here may be an appropriate place to mention a minor trick that made dealing with miniature layouts much easier for me. Such layout sheets often have a scale on one or both sides, so I cut off one of these strips and glue it to the back of my ruler or type gauge. As inches or ems or centimetres are measured on one side of the rule, they can immediately be transferred to the layout by turning the rule over and measuring off the same number on the miniature scale.

A reverse bracket thus,], on the left hand side would show that copy is to be printed flush left and a similar mark on the right, [, would show that copy is to be set flush right, ragged left, but for clarity these instructions, flush left etc. should be written in the margin on the left that is reserved for typesetting instructions.

If you have everything ready at once for page layout, it should be bundled up with dummy pages indicating what is to go where, the positions and sizes of the advertisements marked on the pages, and a list of the stories and filenames if these are not indicated on the pages.

If anything is running a little late, then be sure that as much as can be sent goes on schedule or slightly earlier, with a note of what is to come.

If the pages are laid out in a separate office, it is a good idea to make a list of everything that is sent, and keep a copy so you can check that everything has been set.

Making pages fit

Correction marks — page 134

When the page is completed, or if the work is done outside, the proofs are returned, you may find that some stories run short, and others are too long. It is a good idea to make a separate copy of the proofs so that you can work on these problems while the pages are read for errors. If you are doing the work in-house or yourself, it is also good practise to print out the whole publication at this stage and to work on the hard copy. You will find you work much faster and more surely on paper. You should use the correction marks as shown here (Figure 12-2) or be sure that any departures from these is clearly understood by those who will be doing the work.

If you are doing your own page layouts then some of the following advice will apply directly at that stage rather than in marking what is to be done on the proofs.

Sometimes you may find that an article is a little too long, and you may be tempted to reduce the area set aside for the heading. Remember that such a move will damage the overall appearance of the magazine.

However, you may be able to shift an illustration into the heading area, perhaps even reversing the heading out of the illustration if it has a very dark area, or overlaying the head in black if it has a very light area. Alternatively you may be able to bleed an illustration into the gutter or out to the edge of the page, or to the top or bottom, provided you have confirmed with the printer that this is possible in that position on that particular page.

Your other option is to cut the article — but in this case remember that any cuts other than at the end will involve re-running the text which may affect the positions of crossheads and could create "widows" which are short lines at the tops of columns that are the final line of a paragraph starting in the previous column.

Widows and orphans

There is some confusion over which is which in defining widows and orphans but the most common usage in publication production is that widows are these short lines at the tops of columns and are not to be tolerated. Orphans, which are one line of a paragraph at the bottom of a column are usually allowed.

In some production houses widows are tolerated — but even here the widow which consists of just a hyphenated section of a word will be removed in some way.

Leaving to last

You may find that some widows appear on the proofs, and this may be because the person preparing the page knows that there have to be some alterations and will not spend time adjusting paragraph spacing to remove widows when he or she knows that their position is likely to change.

In many cases a slight adjustment to the tracking of the paragraph, or a previous one, will rid a column top of a widow, either by bringing it back or by forcing another line over. If you can see a word which could be cut to bring a widow back to the previous column, then by all means mark it, but perhaps also mark it as an "optional" alteration so that if other changes make it unnecessary, this change does not need to be made.

Correction required	Mark in text	Mark in margin
Delete	a let̸ter too many	↗
Insert words or punctuation	ʌ is missing	word ʌ
Close up	sp͡ acing is wrong	͡
Leave as printed	not really a mistake	stet
Change to caps	a town in nsw	caps
Change to lower case	it was new to (US)	l.c.
Change to italics	put this in italics	ital
Change to bold	emphasise this	bold
Change to roman	it should not be (bold)	rom
Wrong font	a letter out of place	wf
Replace damaged character	something wrong	X
Transpose	a letter swithced	trs
Insert space	a space needed	#
Reduce space	too much ͡ space	Less #
Indent	⌐ Put in a bit	⊊
Move to right ot left (or centre)	⌐ Move Move ⌐	⊊ or ⊋
Begin new paragraph	an end. Or to begin	n.p.
No fresh par (run on)	an end or a new beginning	run on
Print abbreviation in full	it was (appox) right	spell out
Insert quotation marks	He said: ʌ I said ʌ It was. ʌ	ʺ ʺ ʺ ʺ

Fig.12-2: Examples of the most common marks used in the correction of proofs. These are not the official "standard" marks but those found by the author to be among those in general use.

Corrections

Where misteaks occur

Always be aware that alterations and corrections introduce the possibility of making further errors. There have been classic cases of printed correction paragraphs being reduced to gibberish because of errors — or even of compounding an error where the correction was worked out carefully between lawyers.

At one time, when type was set in slugs of metal, some time would be spent trying to find a word to replace a word that had to be cut because it was an error, so that as few lines as possible would need to be reset. That is no longer necessary, but you should still be aware of what kind of adjustments can and cannot be made so that if you cut a long word from a paragraph, you will at least be aware that this may reduce the number of lines taken by that paragraph, and that this can change the position of all following paragraphs by a line.

You should have checked all dates and other facts at the copy stage, but double check them now, especially to see that any reference to a day and date refer to a possible combination — perhaps you will find that Tuesday September 8 is given but a look at the calendar shows that September 8 is a Friday. Check any calculations and if an article refers to seven people and then names them, count the names to make sure there are seven!

Check too that a badly worded heading has not forced the person doing the page layout to excessively increase or reduce type size or the amount by which the type face has been condensed or expanded. The freedom of such systems can produce some strange appearances if a type is condensed more than about 10 per cent.

Page proofs

Not for second thoughts

Remember that page proofs are intended as proofs to correct mistakes, not as an opportunity to have second thoughts about your layouts. Obviously any disasters will have to be corrected, but otherwise you are generally stuck with what you have. If it doesn't look so good on the page, try to do better next time. Any errors in heading typesetting will need to be corrected, and you should also read through the body type to ensure that sections are in the correct order and that any turns from one page to another do read on as intended. Check all turns from one column to the next and confirm that all continuation lines do indicate the correct page number.

Check that page numbers and any running title and date lines at the head or foot of each page are correct. Even major newspapers have been known to come out with the previous day's date at the head of a page.

Check that the captions refer to the pictures they are next to and that the right picture is in each place — especially with pictures of people. If you are not sure, look at the original. Check that the male and female combination in captions is right. Check every phone number by dialling the number and seeing who answers! Similarly check every web address by typing it into a web browser.

Check that any spelling of a name in a heading is the same as occurs in the body of the story, and that it is the same throughout. Anything that you feel sure "must be right" without checking will be wrong for sure.

Then, you have a last look through for anything you may have missed and send the proofs back to the printer or bureau. In some instances you will receive revised proofs, certainly where any new material has been added but after these are approved, a few days later you will have the exciting experience of looking at the finished work.

With luck, you will not see many errors glaring at you so obviously from the pages, but it is unlikely that the product will be completely error free.

Be prepared for complaints; remember that many people will see what they want to see and not necessarily what is there. You may even find that you are accused of being biased by both sides if you attempt to explain both sides of any argument, and from that you can probably judge that you have achieved your aim.

The editor's day off

I know of editors who cannot be found on the day a publication comes out, so that they do not have to answer irate readers without a warning of what is wrong. However by doing this they also miss the occasional spontaneous praise, which though less common, makes up for many brickbats.

From each issue there will be things to learn — layout ideas that have not quite worked, and occasionally something that has worked better than envisaged, and which you will want to do again.

2: NEWSLETTER

Speed of production

Much of what appeared in the first part of this chapter applies equally to production of a newsletter — or indeed to any kind of publication, including newspapers.

The main difference is one of speed in production which results from newsletters working to more of a production line system. However, the division is blurred by some newsletters being very well designed publications and some magazines being produced to a rigorous format that is closer to that of a newsletter. For the purpose of this chapter, we will follow the production of *The Gumboot Newsletter* as a monthly newsletter of eight pages.

Typically newsletters are more compact and have a formalized column layout that has similar items in the same position each issue.

They are more likely to be produced entirely in a word processing program, but many are also produced using advanced page layout programs. Photographs and other illustrations tend to be included only where they are essential to the content rather than for effect.

In some cases the editor may even type those articles he writes for himself straight into the layout, and will have several formats to cope with articles of different lengths without having to spend much time considering the artistic aspect.

Positioning heads and crossheads

Clash across the columns

Much of what has been described in the previous section still applies — especially to the positioning of headlines on a page, and to the relative fall of crossheads and illustrations. It is a sign of lack of care if crossheads fall next to each other in adjacent columns. Even if such crossheads have to go in a specific position a clash can usually be avoided by moving an illustration, or by making a change to other items such as headings, bylines, introductory paragraphs, breakout etc.

By their nature a newsletter format is likely to result in greater emphasis being given to news, but there is little reason for this other than to take advantage of a shorter production schedule. So, we will start with the same material as in the magazine example.

The advertisements will be positioned on the dummy, but instead of being in specific positions they may well be able to be used as fillers — placed at the bottom of any page where a story falls short. However, if you are moving ads from where they are placed on the original dummy, write them on a "to place" list, or you may find your revenue strangely short, or the advertiser asking why they have received a bill, but no ad.

Where things go

It is probable that the forthcoming gumboot exhibition will be the major news item, and the equivalent of the introduction to the magazine feature will be written with emphasis on what is new and how many exhibitors there are, to lead page one.

As the main feature, the detailed survey of exhibitors may take advantage of the centre-page spread to go across the gutter, if the printer says that this is possible.

The contents details may form a box on page one, with some of the better small news items and a good photograph completing that page.

The president's message may occupy an editorial or leader-like box on page two, perhaps with the secretary's column alongside and the letters underneath.

Page three could feature the collector story, presented again in news-feature style. Pages four and five will have the exhibition feature, and the remaining features will form the page leads on the remaining pages.

Items such as the branch officers and aims will go below these and the remaining news items, instead of being grouped together, are likely to be used as "fillers" wherever they are needed.

There will never be agreement on exactly what a newsletter should look like. Often the major story goes at the top, and then other stories are graded down progressively using smaller headlines until at the foot of the page are small single-column fillers. In other formats items will flow on one after another, with single or double column headings as the items fall.

Headings may be centred or set flush left, and should generally be consistent, although, as with magazine layouts, if the editor or page-layout person is working with a computer, there will be more opportunity to try out various options.

Modular layouts

Squared up stories

Some newsletters opt for a modular layout, in which each article occupies a rectangular space, but it is more normal for successive stories to be butted in partly under the one above, to give a continuing line of sight from one top corner of the page to the opposite bottom corner, the main headings being more or less equally spaced along this line. Introductions may be set to the width of the number of columns in the bottom line of the heading, or may be to single-column width.

In the blurring of definition between newsletters and magazines, it is becoming increasingly common to use bastard measure setting (i.e. non-standard as used for versions of metal files and rasps too!) — perhaps three columns to a part of a page where the normal layout is four columns, and in fact almost all features of magazine layout have been carried across.

The original vertical column format of publications was a product of the engineering by which they were produced. It was necessary to lock-up the metal formes so the suction of paper coming off the forme when it was printed did not carry with it any of the type. Everything was squarely locked between column rules, and even as headlines spread over more than one column and column rules disappeared, it was still necessary to have solid lengths of metal between the columns.

Spacing

Using white

In hot metal days, spacing materials always seemed in short supply, so newspapers were usually mostly solid type, and this has set the general appearance of newsletters as well, even though offset printing freed them from such restrictions and meant that space was available anywhere without problem. Many early newspapers, especially those of a couple of centuries ago, were much smaller in page size and looked much more like our present day newsletters.

Things to avoid in newsletter layout include adjacent headlines that could be read together — one story can be boxed, or turned into a reverse or stipple head, or better still a picture can be used to avoid such heads butting against each other. But if heads have to go next to each other, ensure that they are at least two sizes apart (the largest head going next to a 48 pt head should be a 36 pt one) and in a different style (light against bold, italic against roman).

Also, the page should be designed so that fillers go at the bottom, and not to fill in awkward holes at the ends of stories higher up on the page. That does not mean that small stories should not be used at the top — but if they are, they should be deliberately placed. For example, it is common practice to place a small but important story in a box, or set in bastard measure, above the main story. Similarly, a single column story in the right or left hand column can bring emphasis to something that might be lost further down the page.

Although newsletters tend to follow newspaper practice of grading stories in heading size down the page, there is also a tendency to have only a very small number of size options and to use boxes to add emphasis to a small story.

Pictures

Put the big one at the top

Although we have said that illustrations in newsletters are more usually placed where they are needed for the flow of the story, a main picture should still be in the top half of the page and a second, smaller, picture can strengthen the lower half

If pictures are scanned in a separate operation it is normal to give each picture a reference number that is based on the page number, so the first picture on page 3 will be pic 3/1, the second picture on that page pic 3/2 and so on. You could also use 3A, 3B . . .

If there is any possibility of confusion, as with pictures of people, it is advisable to write not only the name of the person on the layout, but also a description that will ensure no one can pick the wrong one — "man facing right with glasses", "girl with necklace". Also write in the first few words of the caption to again avoid any possible confusion.

Regular logos should be cut out and stuck on the rough layout, even if the file is stored on the computer unless they are used every time in the same place to the same size. If a logo is to be lifted from a previous issue, write in the issue date and page where it was last used.

Working with others

Look and learn

If the newsletter or magazine is being prepared for you at a service bureau, printery or design studio, an experienced sub-editor or layout artist will see most of these points from a look round at the printers. For the less experienced it will be necessary to ask, but any printer or production manager would be well advised to spend some time sorting out such points at the earliest stage. It is also good to have ready a number of filler stories of sizes from one paragraph upwards.

If you are not doing the page layout on computer yourself, the extent that you wish to go to with layouts is largely up to you. You can produce a fully-drawn layout that resembles closely the finished page, even to sketched pictures and shaded reverses. You can, on the other hand, use just outline rectangles to indicate where headings and body copy go, and just write in the first words of heads and the catchlines. It depends very much on what time is available for preparations. If you are not going to be present when the pages are prepared, then a more detailed layout will lead to fewer possibilities of confusion and misunderstanding.

Be consistent

There are just a few established ways of marking what you want on a layout. Where some layout subs will mark in the full rectangle for a picture and put corner-to-corner diagonals across it, others will just put token ticks from each corner. Some will use colored markers to indicate rules, others will use black. The main point is to be consistent within your own layouts.

One point should be made if you do go into the comp room or in a design studio to watch over the layout process — only the craftspeople should handle the working materials, whether disks, film, printouts etc., unless you are clearly told that you can do so. This dates back to the days of print unions being among the most powerful of craft unions, but it is also just good etiquette. The work of a compositor or designer is the work of a skilled craftsperson. No-one should interfere with the tools or work-in-progress of a craftsperson anywhere!

Chapter 13

Paste-up

Old ways still used

Pasting up is no longer common outside playgroups and elementary schools. Most publishers produce complete pages, output to PDF files in readiness for creating film or going direct to the press, and printing to laser printers is usually just for proofing. However paste-up *does* still exist and *is* sometimes very useful particularly to the small newsletter or "zine" publisher who works by printing out page masters on a laser printer then photocopying them. It is a way of making alterations to pages which have been output already or where there are problems in getting a file to output as a whole.

It is also useful for introducing features ranging from pasting in drawings or copied line art, rather than scanning them and placing them on the page in the computer. Another use is creating special effects: there are some things you can do very simply in paste up, such as a shattered effect where you slice up an illustration, or line of type, and paste it down with each slice slightly out of alignment. This can be done with expensive software that takes time to learn, or very simply with a knife and a steel rule.

Therefore, while this section gets smaller with each edition of this book it remains useful for some while also being an introduction of concepts which are the basis for the front end of DTP programs. And, though it tends to be used for a number of "zines" (along with hand drawn headings), may be too uncommon and archaic to survive beyond this edition.

A drafting board or table with a T-square is more than adequate for getting everything squared up correctly, especially if you are producing modular sections. You can draw guidelines in light blue and even get layout sheets printed with columns and page areas marked in light blue. You will also need at least one type gauge or rule, preferably one long and one short, and one of these should be metal to use as a cutting guide.

On the 'stone' or light table

The make-up bench

The make-up bench is usually called the "stone" because in the earliest days of printing that is what it was made of. Later it was made of sheet metal but now that only paper has to be supported, they can be of much lighter construction. A small bench of translucent glass or plastic with fluorescent tubes underneath can also serve for viewing transparencies.

You can make a light table from a cheap secondhand desk which has a damaged top — often seen in secondhand stores for just a few dollars. Cut the top out to accommodate a sheet of frosted glass just a little larger than the page or double page sheets you will be working on, and screw in some battens at the edge to support the glass. Any glass supplier will sand-blast a sheet of heavy-gauge glass (not ordinary window glass, as it won't support your weight).

Under the desk make a framework to hold several short fluorescent fittings, and an electrician will soon wire them in place to a switch on the side of the desk. You may need to put some form of shading under the tubes to stop too much light coming from there. You can use Indian ink to draw the main outline of the page size on a grid.

A plastic cutting board that is marked with dots in the form of a grid can be bought from print supply houses or from many general office suppliers.

Cutting with a knife

Use a break-off section knife to ensure you always have a sharp edge. The major point to remember when cutting with such a knife is to watch where you are going, and not where you have been. That may seem obvious but there is a natural tendency to watch the top of the blade instead of the bottom, which is the part that is cutting. This becomes especially important when cutting around intricate shapes such as for cut-out pictures. However, with a little practise you will be able to follow the most intricate of outlines, and even to add the shape of an edge lost against the background. If you are cutting a straight line you must cut hard against your steel rule.

Waxing machine

If you are going in for large-scale production, you could buy a waxing machine, which uses candle wax to coat the back of artwork to bond it to the paper in such a way that it sticks down but can be lifted off to be repositioned as often as necessary. You may be able to buy a secondhand waxer for a reasonable price as their use diminishes. However, waxers are still being made by companies such as Daige in both benchtop models and smaller handheld units.

The alternative is rubber solution — messy but cheap. On the plus side the ball of dried rubber solution that you will gradually build up from the edges of artwork also serves as a useful eraser and artwork cleaner!

Guidelines in blue

You may want to have layout sheets printed showing page and column outlines, or your printer may be able to supply them. You may consider getting some layout sheets printed with running heads in position (overprinted in black). Light blue pencils will be needed to draw in guidelines that will not show when the page is reproduced.

Assembling pages from individual lines and columns of type which might be set on a laser printer is no longer common, but you may find that knowing how to do it will come in useful for making changes and for remaking pages that have already been typeset. It may also be useful for a quick remake of an existing advertisement or to cope with one which has been made to the wrong size.

Cut squarely around type that you are going to paste down. Edges that are not parallel will give an impression that the actual type is not square.

If you need to cut a word or two off the end of a paragraph, remember to keep the full point, preferably with a good sized piece of blank paper, so that you can move this into the correct position.

Filling the page

Crossheads can be used to fill out a page, or short lengths of display borders or thick plain rules can be used to break up solid columns. If they have to be set with the main copy, it is a good idea to pick them so that they apply to a couple of paragraphs below where you write them in. You will then be able to move them a couple of pars in either direction without them being too far from their source.

Borders were once produced in great variety on rolls of adhesive tape and getting them straight could be a challenge. If a border is needed now it will be more common to reset the story with the border in the computer.

Boxes and borders

'In' a page

I was asked some years ago why publications always referred to "boxes" around type when in fact they are one-dimensional borders. The reason is that in letterpress printing they are boxes — they may not have a bottom or a top but they do have four physical sides of metal. What you were seeing was the image produced by the box. Similarly some publishers still refer to an article as being "in" a page rather than "on" it.

You can also draw borders with any of the drawing pens (Rotring make some of the best) available in any art supply shop. The problem with such pens is that they seem to require more time in cleaning than in actual use. For anything other than the highest quality work, you will be well served by the nylon-tip pens sold as having a specific tip width in fractions of a millimetre.

You will also need a white-out medium to cover mistakes. If you use a lot, you may prefer to go for process white paint, but typewriter correction fluid works well.

For last minute corrections the people who were specialists in such layout were able to lift a word from previous layouts — or even from a printed page. They would look for a row, and remember that letter sequences occur in many words, e.g. 'eat' is also in 'create' and 'theatrical' as well as in 'feat', 'meat' etc.

Keep edges clean

There are still some publications which make up the advertisements separately to the correct size and lift them if they are repeated in future issues. However to avoid the work of cleaning the edges of paste-ups it is usually better to at least print out the whole ad each time it is used.

Incidentally, if you ever get to the stage of assembling words from separate letters, you may notice that if you just try to line up the base of each letter, your line seems very uneven. The reason for this is that to achieve an impression of being in line, the bowls of the rounded letters extend below the base of straight-based letters in most type faces — an 'o' will be slightly below an 'h'; the bottom of the bowl of a 'b' may go slightly below the straight bottom serif of that letter. There are many books on type faces and typography which will explain more of these points.

Admit limitations

Endless options

As you will gather by now, the options in production are almost endless. The biggest problem may be to admit your limitations and the extent to which you may need assistance and training. For example, if you plan to produce your own pages on a laser printer, it may be worthwhile, before you commit yourself to a production system, to produce some sample pages and put them aside for a day or two. Then compare them with pages from publications you would like to emulate. If they don't look as good, then reconsider your system, and perhaps take some lessons at a community college or reconsider the economics of getting more of your work done by professionals.

Many of these principles will also apply if you just wish to produce a piece of artwork for editorial or an advertisement in a publication that is otherwise produced commercially.

There is no mystery about paste-up. The key is accuracy, and that is made easier by preparing as much as possible for direct output of pages from the computer, and, where items have to be pasted-up, in the use of T-squares and/or pre-printed or drawn light blue guide lines. Take every opportunity to watch professionals at work as most printing firms are happy to show someone who is interested around their plant.

Even now it is not unusual to find a paste-up bench in many otherwise computerised printing works or studios.

Chapter 14

Using the software

A brief guide

This chapter will look at production of a publication using some specific computer applications. However it is not intended to be a manual in the use of these programs, rather a brief guide to how they and similar programs work so that you can perhaps decide which to use and know what to look for in training.

To start, we will consider a newsletter produced on a no-frills personal computer, such as may be found in many homes as well as offices and using software that is probably already installed.

This will be the kind of equipment readily available to most clubs without requiring the purchase of special equipment. In this section I will use the most common of word processing programs, Microsoft Word, which is available for PCs and the Apple Macintosh computer.

Secondly, we will move up to some of the programs capable of producing a professional-looking publication, requiring some specialised equipment and specialised programs. In this category you would be involved in expenditure of several thousand dollars. Lastly, we will take a brief look at the kind of equipment you would need to produce a full-scale

Fig.14-1: A simple newsletter can be produced quite easily in Microsoft Word, or most word processors by using section breaks every time there is a change in the number of columns, such as for a heading across multiple columns.

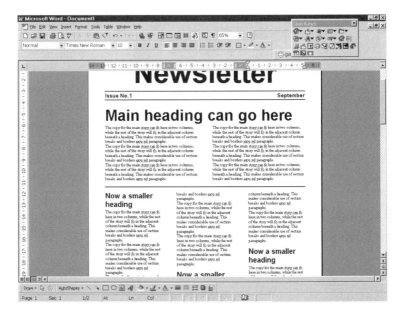

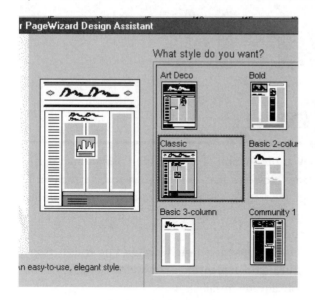

Fig.14-2: For someone who has the job of producing a newsletter without any training, MS Publisher offers a set of "Wizards" which offer many options in layout and then produce a template into which you can drop text and illustrations. It is the instant expert approach but it produces a reasonable result with little effort.

magazine or newspaper, which in most cases is now only a small step from the previous category.

Getting started

Reading the files

You have to produce a newsletter for your service club. You have access to a computer. What do you do? Firstly, try to encourage anyone who is writing for you to give you their contributions on a disk or by e-mail. Most common word processors will read the file formats of other common programs, and it is worth noting that the Apple Mac computer can write and read disks to Windows format; all you have to do is insert a disk that is formatted for Windows and the Mac will read from it and write to it in that format. Another option is to have files sent as e-mail attachments via the internet.

Most domestic scanners also come with software which will read-in text from printed copy and insert it into a word processor file, so there is seldom now the need to depend on finding a skilled typist to hand key all the copy. Remember though that while such software usually claims a 99 per cent accuracy rate it rarely achieves that in practice because of poor quality originals and words such as names with an unusual combination of letters, so you do have to read such scanned copy very carefully.

Use section breaks

Most word processing programs will allow you to set up copy in two or more columns with varying degrees of ease. The methods are so diverse that the only way to find out is a thorough reading of the manual. However in the case of Microsoft Word, the key to doing this is to realize that section breaks are used between items which you wish to span a different number of columns. Thus there will be a section break between a heading across the page and the copy beneath it which runs in two columns, and another section break between that article and the next heading spanning the page and between that and the final story which is in three columns.

From word processor to layout program

There is a substantial jump between word processing programs, and page layout programs. In the latter, rather than relating to how many columns, you place either the text or a frame to hold the text and can drag it to any required width and depth. Few of the programs in this category that we mentioned in our second edition are still around. Instead the low-cost field is headed by another Microsoft program, Publisher, though you should also consider programs such as Ready,Set,Go!, Ragtime and PagePlus. You will find brief descriptions and links to more information on our web site.

The next step up is to programs such as Adobe InDesign and QuarkXPress, though we should not forget Corel Ventura. Adobe PageMaker is still widely used though it has effectively been superseded for newcomers by InDesign. For Linux users there are programs such as TeX and Scribus.

All these programs enable you to set up a page, by specifying the margins, number of columns, line spacing (leading) and a default, or body copy type size. In some you draw frames for the areas where you are going to put type, in others you place the copy direct on to the page and then import illustrations so that the type adjusts around them.

Microsoft Publisher

Complete with templates

For an example of the second category let us look more closely at Microsoft Publisher, the most popular low-cost package.

This program comes with a number of templates for newsletters, several of which are eminently suitable for adapting to magazine use. Even if you plan to create your own design, it is advisable to look first at some of the templates so you can see how these make use of the program's features.

The preparation work is exactly as described in Chapter 12 — and it is still best to draw up a rough layout on paper. Taking this, one calls up the publication file or template (and immediately saves this under another name to avoid making unwanted changes to the master file).

It is advisable, as with all these programs, to save your file frequently — against the possibility of losing work through a power failure or program glitch.

One of the advantages of Publisher is the ease with which you can call in illustrations and change their size and proportions —and that you can do the same thing with type set as a graphic on the page.

But this is not intended to be a manual on these programs — just an indication of how they work.

Another program worthy of consideration which is in this price category, or even less, but which has substantial capabilities is Serif PagePlus.

InDesign

Same on PC or Mac

Let us turn now to InDesign, which is effectively identical on the PC or the Macintosh computer. Again the first job is to design templates. As well as specifying the page size and margins, you can specify a number of columns and the gutter between them, although this can be changed "on-the-fly". You also specify a number of "styles" which are type and spacing specifications that apply to complete paragraphs although they can be easily overridden for selected marked areas of text.

Text is commonly placed one file at a time and positioned on the page by moving and clicking the cursor. It can be run into just one column, or can "autoflow" from one column to the next, and the next, until finished. If you select the type area nodes appear on the light blue frame surrounding the type. You can move the whole type area by clicking and dragging anywhere in the frame and the nodes allow you to reshape the frame. Towards the bottom of the right hand frame edge is a small rectangle. If the story continues in another visible frame this is filled with a small blue arrow head but if the rest of the story is not yet placed, a red plus sign appears. If the rectangle is empty you have the end of the story. Frames can include more than one column and these can automatically adjust as you alter the width of the frame.

It is also possible to drag all the stories and illustrations for a page, or set of pages, by dragging the files from a folder window onto the page.

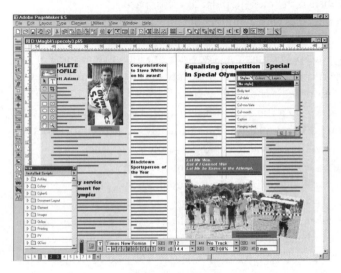

Fig.14-3: A newsletter being prepared in PageMaker. Note the scripts palette at the lower left of the screen, a key to automation in this program.

If you drop them on the pasteboard, for example, they will all import simultaneously one on top of the other, but all there ready to be worked on. Frames do not have to be created ahead of importing text or images though they can be created first, so that you can create a layout before having the items to be used in that layout. In this way you can simulate the comp working on a layout by cutting text and placing it temporarily outside the page area — the only problem being that you may want to invest in a larger screen or second monitor to be able to see the page and all the required palettes at the one time.

Working with frames

QuarkXPress is the program long associated with the production of magazines and also involves the use of frames for text and images, though this tends to be a program where the idea is to plan more fully in advance, creating the frames, specifying what kind of content they will be used for and then filling them.

In Corel Ventura you have a similar job in preparing your page size and margins, and similarly prepare "tags" which specify type and spacing as applied to individual paragraphs, or groups of paragraphs. Instead of placing type on to the page, it is usually placed into frames, which are drawn at the required position and to the required size.

Columns within frames

Frames can have one or several columns, and columns need not be the same widths.

You can specify in advance the system you want to use in adding additional spacing, above and below crossheads, above and below paragraphs and lines of type, so that when the file appears in the frame it will be spaced to fit exactly if this is possible within your guidelines, and columns will be equal in length.

The learning curve

InDesign, XPress, PageMaker and Ventura are extremely complicated programs. They have to be to do everything that can be done with type and even at their complexity they have to compromise on some aspects, so there is a fairly lengthy learning curve. Trial versions are available for most of the programs, but these do not come with manuals, so it is probably better to depend on recommendations from people who will be around to help when you run into difficulties.

It is fairly easy to explain the main points to new users so that one can become productive in a short time — a few hours. Then comes the lengthy period during which you find out how to achieve the effects you want, and to find the easiest way of doing things.

There is no alternative to reading either the manuals or one of the books written about each program — and reading them again and again, for each time you do you will see something that you did not see before. Also, read every magazine article in the specialist press that covers the program you have chosen.

Do not expect to get one of these programs and be able to use it for productive work immediately unless you have an experienced person to guide you. You must allow yourself time — and this is equally true if you are changing from another method of production.

I suggest you do this slowly — perhaps using the new page layout program for just a page or two, or just running type into suitable width columns for pasting up in the old-fashioned way. As you learn, you will be able to do more on the computer without wasting too much time and creating too much stress.

Templates and styles are the key

Make changes slowly

Be prepared to spend time preparing formats, templates or stylesheets — they are the key to efficient production with any of these programs.

On a weekly publication when PageMaker was introduced to replace a dedicated phototypesetting system, the editorial was first run into templates set up for each column width. The heading was typed directly into another template set up with the tighter letter spacing which looks much better in a news heading. Within a few weeks the sub-editors were producing the heading and text in one piece, and within a month or so were producing sections of a modular layout with headings, bylines, text and captions in place and ready for the comps to run through a waxer, trim, and stick down into position on the paste-up.

It was decided that because of the uncertainty of advertisement sizes (especially an unfortunate tendency for typesetters to make ads slightly deeper if they could not fit in all the copy easily!), there would not be an attempt to go to full pagination on the computer until everyone was thoroughly used to how the new process worked.

The advantage of this graduated method of introduction is that there is no sudden change. No one is overawed by the complexity of the software and production speed does not suffer. I have seen some overnight changes to production which have been costly disasters. Don't let salesmen tell you that these systems are simple. They are not, but they can work wonders when you slowly begin to understand them.

In a similar transfer from PageMaker to InDesign, the people doing the page layout started by preparing a few headings and some advertisements in InDesign and then creating EPS or PDF files from these which were placed in PageMaker. As they became more adept using the new software, they switched over to InDesign for the whole process.

In the slow introduction cases mentioned above, the compositors were soon producing advertisement and editorial feature layouts that would previously have required the services of a graphic designer.

Automation

In many layout programs, page layout can be automated. In PageMaker this can be achieved by the built-in scripting language which can be controlled from the script palette or which can also be driven by external programs, via what is known as DDE (dynamic data exchange) on the PC or through Applescript on the Mac. QuarkXPress can be substantially scripted via Applescript on the Mac and InDesign has a variety of scripting options including VisualBasic, Applescript and the cross-platform option of Javascript.

Such automation involves a considerable amount of work but any task which is repeated many times should be considered for this process. If scripting cannot be done in house, there are specialists available who can write scripts to your specification.

Graphics programs

Programs such as Illustrator, FreeHand, CorelDraw or Canvas can be used to create illustrations and to adapt scanned artwork or disk-based clipart. Most such programs also come with a very wide range of type faces and can be quickly used to create single lines of type in special type faces and effects for export in a format such as encapsulated PostScript (EPS) or portable document format (PDF) — this in turn can be imported into the page-layout program. The range of type faces with such programs can be a reason for buying them — to purchase the type faces on their own could cost more.

However, if you are proposing to buy any of these programs, do not do so without seeing it in use and trying your hand at a few basic functions. If the computer firm you are dealing with cannot arrange this, then I suggest you look elsewhere — if they honestly admit that they have little knowledge of the particular program, then a good dealer will still take the time to enquire from his suppliers to put you on to a satisfied customer.

More on graphics — page 85

Most programs are also available as trial downloads from the web sites of the software companies. Be warned however that some of these programs are huge, and you do need either a broadband Internet connection or a lot of patience. In addition the learning curve for all of them is steep, so you need to set aside serious time to evaluating them and, as with layout programs, consider if your choice should be based on what training may be readily available locally.

Word processing

Look at programs with less

For simple newsletter work you may find that a word processing program such as Microsoft Word will do all that you require. You can use a wide range of type faces and sizes and you can put type into multiple columns. You may also preview the overall look of a page or pair of facing pages, and you can call in illustrations.

Because I am using one of the high-end page layout programs, I prefer a straightforward word processor and for a long time used the shareware program PC-Write. I now use another shareware program, NoteTab Pro, which, as well as having a spell check and thesaurus, can be set up with an autocomplete function to expand abbreviations — if you constantly have to type something like the "Mendelvijc's amelioration factor analysis" you may decide to only type mafa and allow the program to complete the phrase for you!

A different kind of copy editor

Two programs work together

In mentioning InDesign as a page layout program, we should also mention its sister program, InCopy. Basically InCopy is a cut-down version of InDesign intended for editing copy which has already been laid into a page. A typical use would be with a magazine which is using Adobe InDesign for layout and where pages or individual page items need to be sent back for editing to fit or for final corrections.

This allows all editing functions either in the layout as seen on the page or in a text editor format but the copy editor is locked out of many or all layout changes and from editing any other parts of the page. It is very different to the standard text editor incorporated into InDesign which just presents the text, and very basic formatting, for editing in a standard size and type face — though that is especially useful if the text is set wide in a small font or is otherwise hard to see in the layout view.

There is a trial version of InCopy on the Adobe web site but be aware that the hardware requirements are fairly high. You'd also need a high speed connection as it is about a 90mb download.

Initially InCopy was only sold by Adobe direct to large scale system integrators (think of the people installing systems for daily newspapers or Condé Nast type magazines) but they have now realized there is a market to any publication which separates the layout and editing tasks.

Search and replace

More than finding text

Find-and-replace, search-and-replace, or find-and-change, as it is variously called, is needed more than one might imagine. It must have the ability to insert non-text items, such as line endings, tabs, and so on, to change double-spaced copy to single spaced, to take out paragraph indent space at the beginning of each paragraph, to insert a blank line between each paragraph, and so on. It is also useful for checking that there are no double spaces between words. You also need to be able to find and replace by font or style, and most programs can do this.

It is useful, for example, to be able to copy (or 'cut' as some programs call it) from the text into the find area. In this way, in getting rid of hard carriage returns at the end of some imported text, I found that these showed up in the find area as ^p in Microsoft Word — something I would never have found in the manual.

Think carefully and you will seldom have to go through copy to make individual changes. If you want to change a single hyphen to a double one for conversion into a dash, then look for space, hyphen, space — or you will be unintentionally changing the hyphen that should remain a hyphen. Similarly, it can be necessary to change something first so that you can make the search-and-replace changes, and then change the original item back.

Scanners

See also page 87

I have mentioned scanners elsewhere, and many of these come with a free cut-down version of a program to change and edit illustration formats. There are many different ways of getting an illustration into digital form, but fortunately most page layout programs are very good at accepting and converting these.

Clipping paths

The program with the scanner may be sufficient but you may find that it lacks essential abilities such as being able to semi-automatically draw around shapes to create cut-outs. (This is achieved by creating what is called a "clipping path" or "mask" around the shape which you want to cut out.)

If you do not have a scanner handy, you may have an ability to receive faxes via a modem attached to the computer. If so, you can send logos and other simple artwork from a standard fax machine to your fax-card-equipped computer and most fax programs will convert the received file into a format which other graphics programs can convert to one which can be used by page-layout programs.

Dots per inch

Different meanings of 'dot'

I should also explain here the difference between the various meanings of "dots per inch". You may wonder why laser printer output at 600 dpi (360,000 dots to the square inch) cannot match the quality of traditional halftones at 100 lpi (around 10,000 dots to the square inch). This is because the laser dots are fixed in size, whereas the halftone dots are variable.

A way to overcome this is to make each group of dots from the laser printer act as one dot from the photographically produced halftone. Various patterns of, say, five dots, can resemble a range of sizes of a halftone dot. There are many ways in which this can be achieved — the more dots you have in a group, the greater the range of greys you can create, but the coarser the overall screen will appear. Your software and laser printer do this work for you.

Tables of contents

Other uses

Most page layout programs have a table-of-contents feature which is primarily intended for book use. However, this feature can also be used for contents lists in magazines and newsletters, usually by requiring the user to mark which style tags are applied to those headings you wish to list in the contents. You can then move items around and recompile the contents list as you go to keep track that everything is included. You can include multiple files via a "book" feature to have the table of contents compile over several files.

However there is another use for such features and that is to compile an index to advertisers. To achieve this, specify a tag that is applied only to the name of advertisers in the layout or include a non-printing line with the name of the advertiser in each advertisement. Such an index will make the advertisers happy — and think how much time you will save in trying to find a particular advertisement in a back issue!

Chapter 15

The e-zine

A presence on the Web

Many publications now exist only on the World Wide Web of the Internet. However, that is not our subject here. What we shall be covering is the web page or rather series of pages which give an electronic presence to a print publication.

This in itself can take many forms.

With a simple newsletter, it can be a decision to produce an exact copy of the print edition using HTML, the web formatting language which produces 99 per cent of the web pages you see. Microsoft Word can do this, but is often criticized for producing excessively complex HTML code. However the choices of type and heading sizes for a simple newsletter are usually fairly limited and there are few complex illustrations, so this can work quite well regardless.

It may be necessary to make some changes to the layout before converting to the format needed for the web — such as changing from multiple columns to a single column format.

To put your "print" newsletter, zine or magazine on the web, exactly as is, the answer is a screen definition PDF which can be downloaded for reading offline with the free Adobe Reader software or viewed on screen provided they have a PDF plug-in installed for their browser software.

In preparing a PDF be aware that there is a big difference in the specifications for on screen use compared with a file which is to be printed. This has little effect on the type but involves mainly the resolution of the graphics — those intended for screen viewing only can be considerably coarser than those for print, dramatically reducing file size.

The whole or part

There are still discussions as to whether it is better to provide the full text of publications on line or to provide an easy means of downloading the whole.

In some cases an answer may be to provide a summary in a form which can be browsed on line and the full text of either the whole or of sections, to be downloaded.

You have to make similar decisions with a publication produced using more advanced page layout software, although increasingly these are being updated to provide easier conversion to formats suitable for the web. Again, however, you have to decide whether you need the full text on line. Some publications have decided that as the full text on line may reduce sales of the print version, that it is better to include only some of the content, and mainly in summary form.

Advertisers

What do they want?

Consideration also has to be given to the advertisers. Are they to receive advertisements in the online version — or a listing in an on-line directory of suppliers? Will this be provided automatically or at extra cost — or only if they request it? Will you provide links to advertisers' own web sites?

At present there are more questions than answers.

In the period since the previous edition of this book we have seen many publishers launch web sites with much fanfare and then quietly drop them or reduce them to a simple announcement and contact details site.

We are still in a stage that it is difficult to quantify benefits from a web page, but one can quite easily see that if a publication does not have a web page it may be considered to be "behind the times". Many readers will now expect to find at least some information available on line, and some publications are using it for the kind of information which they previously included but which was of interest to only a small proportion of their readers.

The answer is probably that a web site can be a great advantage to a print publication but that the costs need to be watched very carefully. If you can do it on a shoestring then the chances of success are greater.

Details not in the print edition

Detailed results or entry listings for contests in the field your publication covers have usually been printed in the smallest of type sizes because those people who are interested will read them with a magnifying glass if necessary, but they are often of insufficient general interest to warrant the cost of the space they occupy.

Now, the answer may be to offer only the major results in the publication and give full details on a web page. If results are available from the organizers, it can, with a little thought, and perhaps a little one-off computer programming, be possible to provide them on line even before the issue is published.

Classifieds and events

Similarly, a web page could be an answer to the problem monthly publications have in getting classified advertisements, particularly for-sale advertisements. An advertiser might have had to wait weeks for the ad to appear. Now, as a combined offer, they can have an advertisement in print, and on the web, with the web advertisement appearing almost instantly. If the price covers both media as one deal, it does not matter if the item is sold before the paper is published and the print ad can be withdrawn if time permits.

Similarly, news of coming events can be kept up to date and an item in the publication may say, "see the web page for any changes".

E-mail newsletters

Mailing lists

A less ambitious form of publication can exist entirely via e-mail. Many e-mail programs allow you to set up mailing lists so that you can send a regular e-mail newsletter to all those on the list. Such newsletters are best composed of a number of small items and display is generally limited, although now that most e-mail programs also recognise the HTML coding that is used for web pages, it is also possible to have increased sizes for headings and to even use color for headings and to emphasise text.

If your distribution increases, sending your own newsletter and managing the distribution list becomes cumbersome and this will be a good time to ask your Internet service provider whether they offer a mailing list service.

These are often used for "e-mail lists" where anyone can send a message and it goes to all the members of the list. However they are equally suited to the closed circulation list, where any messages to the list go to the list owner for editing and possible inclusion. My own *Format* newsletter operates on this basis. At the time of writing this list had around 2000 "subscribers" in well over 60 countries. The central listserver computer handles all subscription requests and cancellations automatically.

All that is involved in sending out the newsletter is to prepare one copy which is e-mailed to the list computer with the access password. Within a matter of minutes it is on its way to all 2000 subscribers.

At one time such services were offered free. Now the service provider may make a charge or reserve the right to add advertisements to each message — which may be acceptable provided you know what kinds of advertisements will be accepted.

Blogs

On-line diaries

A relative newcomer to the Internet are Blogs, a name which derives from weB LOGS, in other words on-line diaries or logs which have comments and descriptions added on an almost daily basis, with the new entries going at the beginning of the file. There is specialist blog software available which allows readers to add comments, somewhat like a message board.

There are blogs maintained by companies, but they tend to be better as personal comments and this is what most blog readers expect. However, they could serve as an alternative to the online newsletter.

Web edition

Exporting from a print program

Another consideration is preparing a web edition of a print publication. This can be carried out in many ways. The easiest is to prepare a web page design with space for a number of stories and pictures to be slotted in, and then export the text and pictures from your page layout program. While there are many criticisms of the web conversion capabilities of PageMaker, for example, this does have the ability to export photographs in the compressed lower resolution formats needed for a web page and exporting text, even as a text file, does ensure that the version used on the web page is the same edited version as used in print. InDesign and QuarkXPress also have capabilities to create web pages from their print files, but there is a requirement to do this following a strict system.

However, while advanced page layout programs may give the ability to export a page to the web which looks exactly like the print version, one has to ask whether this is needed. Someone browsing the web will have entirely different requirements to the casual print reader.

As already noted, a copy of the print edition may be prepared as a PDF file, but the reader will then have to download an entire edition to view an item on one page. A compromise might be to create PDFs of individual pages or features, and to have an HTML page serving as an index, maybe with a brief summary of what is in each PDF file.

Need to reduce image settings

Remember that there are special settings for making PDFs which are suitable for viewing on the Internet which are usually defined as being "on screen" or "e book" settings. However, if you have many illustrations you may find that even these settings produce files which are too large for convenient downloads, especially on dial-up connections. The answer here is to reduce the image settings and in particular the setting for "downsampling images above ... pixels per inch" which really does mean that images below that resolution are not downsampled, so start reducing that figure too. It is a case of trading off size for picture quality and it is surprising how low you can go if all you have to do is create an impression of what the print version looks like.

It can also be useful to split it into several PDFs — though they may add up to slightly more in total size, it is amazing how the impression of slowness disappears when they can be looking at the first one while continuing to download the rest.

Some publishers also see the web edition as being more useful in offering summaries of the major stories together with full details of items such as perhaps classifieds, death notices and so on, where someone wants instant access. The web page can also be useful on breaking stories with up-to-date information.

Start small

Your first step may be to look at the pages offered by a variety of publications and see which kind seems right for you. One consideration will be that while it is always possible to expand a web site, it is much harder to admit that you bit off more than you could chew and reduce the information and services available.

There were very few web sites which have made a profit for publishers. However there are ways of using web sites to enhance the print edition and show that the publisher is aware of a changing world. One magazine we know includes an advertisement on its web site for all advertisers in its print edition who have ads above a certain size, This has proved to be a successful bonus helping to ensure advertisers maintain a regular presence in the publication.

Still to come are practical ways of being able to target the same information at different uses. XML (extensible markup language) holds hope in that editorial could be prepared in a single form and then the XML codes understood to have the required meanings to produce a different end result in a web page or print page layout program.

Spam, e-mail and responses

Keeping in touch with readers

One of the problems with web sites is that if you want contact from readers, you probably need to include your e-mail address, but making this public in this way can invite a barrage of "spam", uninvited and often offensive bulk e-mail which can overwhelm any attempts to deal with the genuine messages.

At the time this was written there were attempts to deal with spam in several ways, including making it illegal and producing software which attempts to distinguish the unwanted from the wanted. Many web and e-mail hosting services now offer spam filtering but it is still a good idea to avoid anything publicizing your e-mail address which originates from your web site.

It should be possible in most code to "munge" the address by using hex or decimal code in place of ascii characters, which at least makes it harder to harvest addresses or to feed the address to the code from a javascript which munges the address. I found several free javascripts to do this but discarded them when I moved to the next method.

I'm changing over forms on our site to use a cgi e-mail program which takes the information on where to send, subject line, etc., from a text file hidden in the cgi folder where it can be accessed only by the cgi script that is also in that hidden folder. These scripts use an e-mail address which is exclusive for this purpose and so far has had no spam at all.

Prior to this I used a specific e-mail address coupled with specific subject lines set up as part of the e-mail address. All e-mail to that address without that subject line was dumped. As these addresses became known I dumped them — you can now guarantee that e-mail sent to o@worsleypress.com will be dumped, which is more than half way through the alphabet, but such 'dumpable' addresses are lasting longer.

Another possibility is to make all references to e-mail addresses into graphics. Those wishing to contact you have to type out your address, but most sincere, human respondents won't mind that, and you can hope they type it correctly.

This is an area where software and other methods change rapidly, so this reference is primarily intended to persuade you that if you are setting up a web site that such points must be considered, and considered in the earliest stages.

Testing an idea

Finding a new niche

One aspect of e-mail newsletters, blogs and web sites which should be considered is that they provide a good means of testing ideas for publications, particularly in smaller scale or niche publishing.

Questions posted to our web site and our e-mail newsletters are used in part to create those newsletters, resulting in comments and suggestions from others who have dealt with similar matters. Then the content of the newsletters forms the additional material and changes for the next editions of our books. As an example, this section of this chapter resulted directly from comments received in this way. The next step might be to turn one or more of those e-mail newsletters into a fully fledged magazine.

For a web site based on an existing magazine, the comments might be used to compile one or more books in fields associated with the magazine which could then be marketed in part through the magazine.

In such a way the publisher gets to own their niche or at least to get a strong foothold without taking too many risks.

Chapter 16

Economics

Ways to get an income

As we mentioned in our chapter on advertisements, the income for a magazine or newsletter can be from either advertisements or copy sales or from both. Some publications derive their entire income from advertisements and are given away free, either generally or to a very specific market. The latter are known as "controlled circulation" publications; they may be free but you have to fulfill certain conditions to receive them — in other words you have to be a potential customer for the advertisers.

The result of a general dependence on advertisements means that publications which do not take ads will seem very expensive in comparison, even though they do not have to print the extra pages on which those ads would appear.

This has changed a little with the acceptance of higher prices for specialised hobby magazines.

Fixed and variable costs

Two selling prices

In most products, there is a fixed cost (all the general overheads and costs leading to the first production item) and a variable cost (the cost of producing the quantity required). The total of these, divided by the quantity produced gives the cost per item, and then you add the profit needed and arrive at a selling price.

With a magazine, you have two selling prices, the cover price of the magazine and the price of advertisements, and a change to the price of the advertisements could change their quantity and relative proportion (the number of double-page spreads or eighth pages for example), both of which can change the bulk of the publication and therefore affect the overall cost of production. This large number of variables can cause headaches in costing.

In fact, I suggest that the computer program you need more than any of the others mentioned in this book is your spreadsheet program.

You are producing a product with more variables than almost any other so you need to get them under control. There are many good books available on how to start a small business, so this chapter will deal only with aspects that are peculiar to publications.

In Chapter 3 on Advertisements we looked at how the inclusion of advertisements will increase overall costs, but should considerably more than cover those extra costs.

Ads: not a panacea

However, this should come with a warning: advertisement revenue is not a panacea for newsletters having problems with costs. If you have a small newsletter currently without advertisements, are you prepared to give up the editorial space taken by advertisements? For example, an 8-page newsletter might gain the equivalent of a full page of advertisements but that effectively means you now have seven pages for your readers and for the "social good" of their activities.

You would either have to charge a very high rate, gain at least three pages of ads, or actually dramatically increase your printing, distribution and production costs to produce 12 pages. In such a case each advertisement would have to bring in the total cost of the space it occupies but at least the same again to contribute towards overall costs. Work through the budget planning below and the ad rates guidelines in Chapter 3 very carefully. As part of this calculate the costs of someone selling the space and that selling space is not an easy task.

You may decide that a compromise is to accept ads only from those who really want to reach your readers and who will come to you. A special interest not-for-profit group might consider page sponsorship as a possibility, perhaps with a strip along the bottom of each page, where the advertiser expresses support for the objects of the group and is said to be sponsoring that page. This may be part of an agreement covering support in other ways too.

Consider again the meeting notice which is to become a club newsletter and we can look at a balance sheet. The cost of paper used will be about the same. Extra cost is the covers, while we have a saving on postage and an income from advertisements. If wrappers replace envelopes, there will be a saving there, unless using wrappers increases the postage rate.

The wrappers will need to carry the name of the publication, the registration details and a return address, together with a postage-paid symbol, but all this can be photocopied, put on with a rubber stamp, or printed at the same time as the address if you are using a computer.

Setting a budget

Items to track

As the publication moves up the scale, let us look at other costs. Here is a list of items to budget for. Some may apply, some may not, but do not ignore the small items as they can jointly add up to a lot.

Printing: printing (machining), collating, binding, packing and delivery.